Fruitful Living

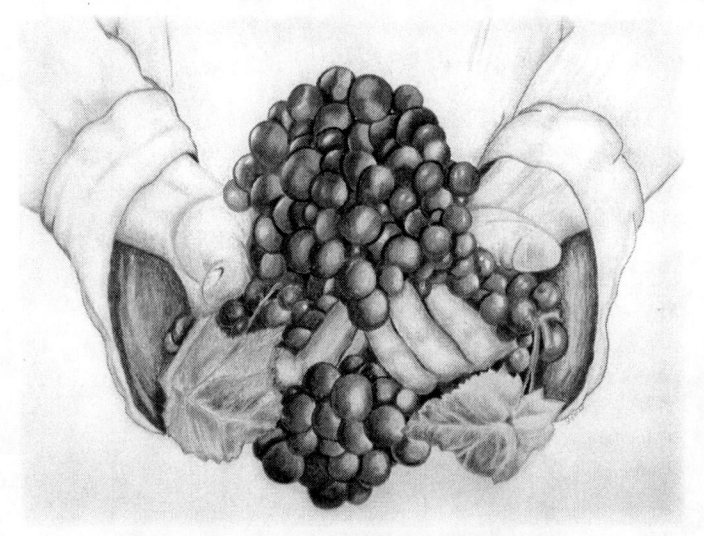

"When you bear (produce) much fruit,
My Father is honored and glorified;
and you show and prove yourselves
to be true followers of Mine.

John 14:8 (Amplified)

Dava Lee Russell

authorHOUSE®

AuthorHouse™
1663 Liberty Drive
Bloomington, IN 47403
www.authorhouse.com
Phone: 1-800-839-8640

© *2009 Dava Lee Russell. All rights reserved.*

No part of this book may be reproduced, stored in a retrieval system, or transmitted by any means without the written permission of the author.

First published by AuthorHouse   11/21/2009

ISBN: 978-1-4490-2738-4 (e)
ISBN: 978-1-4490-2737-7 (sc)

Library of Congress Control Number: 2009912496

Printed in the United States of America
Bloomington, Indiana

This book is printed on acid-free paper.

Scripture taken from THE AMPLIFIED BIBLE, Old Testament Copyright © 1965, 1987 by the Zondervan Corporation. The Amplified New Testament copyright © 1958, 1987 by The Lockman Foundation. Used by permission.

Scripture taken from /The Message/. Copyright © 1993, 1994, 1995, 1996, 2000, 2001, 2002. Used by permission of NavPress Publishing Group.

Scripture taken from the HOLY BIBLE, REVISED STANDARD VERSION. Copyright © 1881-1885, 1901, 1946-1952, 1971. Used by permission of Zondervan Publishing House. All rights reserved.

Scripture taken from the King James Version.

Cover Design: *Jason Britton*
Title Page Art: *Gerald Jones*
Editors: *Donna Renfro, Dava Lee Russell, Ginger Christian, Jason Britton*

Dedication

I would like to dedicate this work to my husband John Russell, who has been my best friend, my co-worker in the Kingdom of God, the outstanding Father to our children, and a man of God full of character, truth, and love.

Thank you, Lord, for the gift of John Russell in my life. Not only have You changed me through his love, but you have melted our hearts together as one. We give You honor and glory for bringing our lives together in Your perfect plan and purpose. Amen!

Introduction

Writing these devotionals on the fruit of the Spirit from Galatians has been a sheer delight in my life. Through the years of walking closely with the Lord, studying His Word, and spending time in His presence, He has truly changed me. As a child, I felt insecure, rejected, and ugly. I use to say, "I have a name like Dava Lee. I'm ugly and I wear glasses, not to mention I am terribly clumsy." You can see my opinion of myself was not very high.

However, as the Lord began to change my life when I received salvation at the age of thirteen, He showed me His love and how much He wanted me to be a strong, happy, fulfilled person. I immediately had a hunger to read my Bible and learn to understand what His Word meant. Even though I was side-tracked by college life and hard studying, I knew I was a child of God. My confidence grew but my self-esteem needed much work. In 1970 the truth of the power of the Holy Spirit of God was shared with me. Once that truth became a part of my heart, my life took on a brand new dimension – one in which God had free reign to change me from the inside out. Truly that is what His love is all about.

Jesus Christ, the only resurrected Son of Jehovah, came to earth so that He might live, die and resurrect from death in order for me to have a full, abundant life while living on the earth. *(John 10:10)* As I began to grasp the Holy Spirit was sent to live in me so that the same power that raised Christ Jesus from the death could dwell in me, my declarations about myself changed drastically. My pastor taught me to pray *Ephesians 1:15-23* substituting my name in the prayer.

[15]For this reason, because I have heard of your faith in the Lord Jesus and your love toward all the saints (the people of God), [16]I do not cease to give thanks for you, making mention of you in my prayers. [17][For I always pray to] the God of our Lord Jesus Christ, the Father of glory, that He may grant you a spirit of wisdom and revelation [of insight into mysteries and secrets] in the [deep and intimate] knowledge of Him, [18]By having the eyes of your heart flooded with light, so that you can know and understand the hope to which He has called you, and how rich is His glorious inheritance in the saints (His set-apart ones), [19]And [so that you can know and understand] what is the immeasurable and unlimited and surpassing greatness of His power in and for us who believe, as demonstrated in the working of His mighty strength, [20]Which He exerted in Christ when He raised Him from the dead and seated Him at His [own] right hand in the heavenly [places], [21]Far above all rule and authority and power and dominion and every name that is named [above every title that can be conferred], not only in this age and in this world, but also in the age and the world which are to come. [22]And He has put all things under His feet and has appointed Him the universal and supreme Head of the church [a headship exercised throughout the church], [23]Which is His body, the fullness of Him Who fills all in all [for in that body lives the full measure of Him Who makes everything complete, and Who fills everything everywhere with Himself]. (Amplified Bible)

Wow! My life turned around. As a result of Bible study and diligently seeking the Lord God daily, the fruit of His Spirit came alive in me. Learning to live my life according to the Word of God, practicing His precepts, and being willing for Him to be Lord of my life were all factors in my growth. By the way, through the years I have also used this prayer in praying for each of our children, grandchildren and other family members. God is powerful in the lives of those we lift to Him in prayer using His Word.

The Apostle Peter tells us in his second letter in the New Testament that Christian growth is a process. Each step helps to bring about the next:

"His divine power has granted to us all things that pertain to life and godliness, through the knowledge of him who called us to his own glory and excellence, by which he has granted to us his precious and very great promises, that through these you may escape from the corruption that is in the world because of passion and become partakers of the divine nature. For this very reason make every effort to supplement your faith with virtue, and virtue with knowledge, and knowledge with self-control, and self-control with steadfastness, and steadfastness, with godliness, and godliness with brotherly affection and brotherly affection with love. For if these things are yours and abound, they keep you from being ineffective or unfruitful in the knowledge of our Lord Jesus Christ. For whoever lacks these things is blind and shortsighted and has forgotten that he was cleansed from his old sins. Therefore, brethren, be the more zealous to confirm your call and election, for if you do this you will never fall; so there will be richly provided for you an entrance into the eternal kingdom of our Lord and Savior Jesus Christ. I Peter 1:3-11 (RSV)

Step by step He leads us. Our decision is to be obedient to His call, open to His teaching, and willing to lay down the old way of life to walk in the newness of His presence every day.

Fruitful Living is a devotional about walking in the fruit of the Holy Spirit of God. None of us has arrived in the perfection of that walk, but all of us have the opportunity to stretch our faith, our obedience, our lives, and our surrender to Him daily in order to literally be filled with the Holy Spirit of God Almighty to walk in victory in every day.

Following each exhortation is some space before the prayer. May I challenge you to take a few moments to write your own feelings about the scripture verses given each day? In learning to journal my own thoughts about what God was saying to me through the years, my faith has grown as I have learned to spend time listening to what the Spirit of the Lord was saying to me. In this ninety-day journey, you will form habits that will carry you through life. When I first began spending quality time with the Lord at the beginning of each day, the discipline became a way of life. Now, I do not feel complete without passing time with Father during the day. Hopefully, you'll find that to be true as well.

My prayer is that these devotional readings on the fruit of the Spirit will encourage you to practice *love, joy, peace, patience, kindness, goodness, faithfulness, gentleness,* and *self-control* in every area of your life. Sharing some examples of each fruit has given me opportunity to see that God is still working on me to change me to be more like Him every day. After all, practice, practice, practice is what life is all about.

Enjoy the journey!

Love

"But the fruit of the Spirit is love..."

Galatians 5:22

Love

This morning when I awakened I lay in bed talking to the Lord, sharing my heart and listening to His. The word **LOVE** kept repeating itself to me.

> **L**ots
> **O**f
> **V**ictory
> **E**ternally

. . . came so clearly to my mind that I had to ponder the thought further. If Christ had not come to earth as a baby in a manger, I could not experience the **Victory** of that **LOVE**! If He had not gone into hell to defeat the devil once and for all, I could not experience **Victory** in my daily walk. If He had not resurrected from the dead, I could not experience His **Victory eternally**!

Now, think about what has you bogged down in light of that kind of powerful **LOVE**. Allow His **LOVE** to flow over you in this moment and know that He came to give you life abundantly right now. *(John 10:10)*

Prayer for the Day

Let's pray the prayer of Ephesians 3:17-20 (RSV paraphrased) . . . according to the riches of his glory he may grant us to be strengthened with might through his Spirit in the **inner man***, and that Christ may dwell in our hearts through faith; that we, being rooted and grounded in* **LOVE***, may have power to comprehend with all the saints what is the breadth and length and height and depth, and to know the* **LOVE** *of Christ which surpasses knowledge, that we may be filled with all the fullness of God. Amen!*

Have a **LOVE***-filled day!*

Love Continued

"Go after a life of love as if your life depended on it - because it does."
I Corinthians 14:1 (The Message)

When we are thinking about **love,** one of the responses from you was "I had a real experience with God this past week as I truly felt His **love poured out over me**." The person went on to explain: "He spoke to me about **LOVE** and how much He has given me and what I am supposed to do with it. While I may not have monetary riches, I have been given an abundance of **LOVE,** and when you have been blessed with the spirit of **LOVE,** you are supposed to go out into the world and give it away."

As we contemplate the **love of God** poured out upon the earth through His Son Jesus Christ, we stand amazed at what manner of **love** the Father has given unto us. *(I John 3:1)* Also, I am overcome with the **love of Christ** for the people around me. I want them to know HIM as I have been privileged to experience His **love**. I want others to see HIM as He really is - full of compassion, holding us close to Himself, and filling us afresh each day as we offer our lives to Him as a "living sacrifice of **love**." *(Rom. 12:1-2)*

Today as we go our separate places of "**love building**," let's pray for one another that we may be filled with His grace to share His **love** with all we touch during THIS DAY!

Prayer for the Day

*May the shining light of Jesus Christ show forth from our lives in order to spread a **"love bath"** upon the world where we walk! Amen!*

Perfect Love

> *"There is no fear in love; but perfect love casteth out fear: because fear hath torment. He that feareth is not made perfect in love."*
> **I John 4:18 (KJV)**

In today's world we are faced with many challenges - often ones of doubt and fear to try to rob us of our **peace** in the Name of Jesus Christ of Nazareth. It is but a choice to believe and remain in His love rather than take up the mental torment of doubt and fear. You may say, "That's easy for you to say." But I tell you I have to make the same choices you have to make each day.

I choose to believe God is **BIGGER** than the challenges of today. God is **GREATER** than any fear that tries to come upon us. God is **MORE THAN ENOUGH** in the midst of a world that tries to convince us we're lacking because of prices, diseases, children in trouble, job loss, etc. God is **MORE THAN FAITHFUL**. He loves with a **PERFECT LOVE**!

Prayer for the Day

*Father, we receive Your **LOVE** afresh and anew today. Allow our minds to dwell on Your **love** and not give in to any fear. We know **YOUR LOVE IS PERFECT**! Amen!*

Revolutionary Love

"I am the good shepherd; I know my own and my own know me as the Father knows me and I know the Father; and I lay down my life for the sheep."
John 10:13-14 (RSV)

When a friend called to tell us that his mission trip was called "Revolutionary Love," my thoughts immediately went to the book of Acts where all the disciples were called to lay down their lives and carry the message of the gospel of Jesus Christ as far as possible. However, as I have meditated upon that thought, all I can think is Jesus not only told us to lay down our lives for our friends, but He gave us the most powerful example of that *revolutionary love* as he poured out his life upon the face of the earth - through the training of his disciples, through addressing the Sanhedrin, through the love He showered on the people through healing, teaching, touching, and proclaiming His Father's message . . .

Today as we walk through our own world, let's be reminded we are fulfilling His *revolutionary love* as we carry His light into the darkness. How can we love with that same *revolutionary* flavor? How can we touch the lives of everyone we contact with the Life Source of His Revolutionary Love? Why not think of someone today to bless with the *revolutionary love* of God?

Prayer for the Day

Father, help me be the carrier of such life-changing love so that everyone I touch today will sense your love! Amen!

Revolutionary Love 2

*"This is my commandment, that ye love
one another, as I have loved you.
Greater love hath no man than this; that a
man **lay down his life** for his friends."*
John 15:12-13 (RSV)

The more I meditate on ***revolutionary love***, the more I sense God's calling His people to a sacrificial giving of ourselves to Him each day of our lives. Often we find ourselves laying down our lives for our family members, but Jesus gave His life for every human being. We too as believers are called to love not only those who are lovely to us but also the ones outside our inner circle for the Kingdom of God to spread.

Jesus Himself certainly lay down His life for us as we read earlier this week. In this passage from John, He exhorted His disciples that as they obeyed what He told them, He called them "friends." *(John 10:14)* When we recognize ourselves as His friends, we can contemplate the reality of true friendship. How precious is His love for us! How magnificent His gift of life!

Prayer for the Day

*Thank you, Father God, for giving us Your precious Son so that each of us can live abundantly upon the earth. Use me today as a friend to those around me who are hurting to carry your **revolutionary love**. May Your life and light shine through me to bless the lives of others! Amen!*

Revolutionary Love 3

*"**Beloved, let us love one another**; for
love [springs] from God, and
he who loves [his fellow men] is
begotten (born) of God and
is coming (progressively) to know and understand God –
to perceive and recognize and get a better
and clearer knowledge of Him."*
I John 4:7 (AMP)

What does it mean to be a **revolutionary**? To me it means one who has a cause and will do anything to see a purpose fulfilled. In our lives as Christians, we have a call to the cause of Jesus Christ and His life's challenge to go into the entire world to carry His gospel. He was very specific in the last chapter of Matthew.

As we come to KNOW Him better, we want to SERVE Him with all our hearts. In order to do that, we must "love one another." There are always people coming our way we may not "like," but the command tells us to "love" one another. The only way we can truly do that is to appropriate HIS LOVE IN US FOR THOSE WITH WHOM WE COME IN CONTACT. Then we are filled with His love and can act accordingly - not from our own "feelings" but from HIS REALITY. This is being a **revolutionary** - one who can cause change in the world around us.

Prayer for the Day

Lord Jesus, grant me Your love! Pour through me with Your goodness, grace and compassion that I look at the people You send my way through Your eyes. Fill me with Your LOVE so that I may love as You love me! Amen!

Revolutionary Love 4

"My little children, let us not love in word, neither in tongue; but in deed and in truth."
I John 3:18 (RSV)

There's a sign in the great room at Buffalo Mountain Retreat Center that reads "Share the gospel often, and if necessary use words" or something to that effect. As I ponder the word of the Lord in I John 3, I am reminded that much of what we do to share love comes through our actions, our sharing, as well as our pouring out good will to others. More people are won to the Kingdom of God through the example we live before them than by being convinced through words.

My Godly Mother always said, "More things are caught than taught." She was a very wise lady! Through the years teaching in a public classroom, the realization that more things are caught than taught really began a part of how I dealt with students. God gave me ways to be a demonstration of His love in the earth rather than just say, "I love you."

As we go through our day, let us find ways to love others by taking a moment to write a note or by smiling at someone who appears lonely or by encouraging a friend to step out into the sunshine for a few minutes to smell the roses. God is in every kind action we give away . . . Have fun sharing the "Sonshine" today!

Prayer for the Day

Thank you, Lord Jesus, for the blessing of giving Your love to others as we go along the day-to-day path of life. Amen!

Revolutionary Love 5

*"No man hath seen God at any time.
If we love one another, God dwelleth in us,
and his love is perfected in us.
Hereby know we that we dwell in him,
and he in us, because he hath given us of his Spirit."*
I John 4:12-13 (KJV)

As we continue to meditate on the revolutionary love of the Father through Jesus Christ, we stand amazed at His goodness to us. Each day as Jesus taught His disciples, He was showing them "love personified." Even when He rebuked the money changers and corrected the Pharisees and Sadducees, He was using the love of the Father because true discipline in love calls for correction at times.

When the living Spirit of Jesus Christ dwells in us, we can love others through His power. As we love the people around us, many are won to the gospel of Jesus Christ. We are seed sowers. We must sow seeds of love and acceptance to those with whom we come in contact. John says no one has seen God, but if God dwells in us, we will love one another and **His LOVE is PERFECTED** in us.

We may have a long way to go to be totally perfected, but today is the first day of the rest of our lives . . . so the journey begins in a fresh new way as we determine to show the love of Christ to all we touch.

What a glorious opportunity to be able to love as Christ loved us!

Prayer for the Day

Thank you, Father, for allowing me to be a part of "a revolutionary love army." Amen!

Revolutionary Love 6

"And Jesus came and spake unto them, saying, 'All power is given unto me in heaven and in earth. Go ye therefore, and teach all nations, baptizing them in the name of the Father, and of the Son, and of the Holy Ghost: Teaching them to observe all things whatsoever I have commanded you: and, lo, I am with you always, even unto the end of the world.'"
Matthew 28:18-20 (KJV)

As we go forth each day with *revolutionary love* in our hearts and a purpose to share love with everyone we come in contact, we are fulfilling the **greatest commission** ever given. Our mission field is right where we are - being living examples of Christ Jesus upon the face of the earth. Keep in mind these were the final teachings of Jesus to His disciples. Many times final words carry more power in the lives of the hearers. He wanted to make certain we fully understood His purpose in coming to earth.

Of course, many go into the foreign mission field, but sometimes our own job place seems like a foreign field because once we come into the Kingdom of God, the world is strange all around us. However, if we do not go and share His love, who will? He told us to go. We must go in His grace, filled with His love and compassion, to fulfill His mandate upon our lives everywhere we walk.

Prayer for the Day

*Thank you, Lord Jesus, for including us as Your disciples upon the earth. Use us this day to impact our world with Your great and mighty **revolutionary love**. Amen!*

Revolutionary Love 7

From I John 3:1 there is a chorus we use to sing often in home Bible studies:

> *Behold, what manner of love the Father hath bestowed upon us!*
> Behold, what manner of love the Father hath bestowed upon us!
> That we should be called the children of God!
> That we should be called the children of God!

Our friend returned safely from the mission to the Czech Republic. PTL! One of the young men in his crew left for the mission field with great problems – home life, drugs, lack of self worth, etc. - BUT GOD met him there through the love that was shared with him by several God-fearing men and youth over the last year or so. During this last week, he met Jesus Christ as his own personal Savior! Our friend was privileged to be one of the men who could love this young man right where he was and share the grace of God through his natural God-given talents.

This morning I was reminded of what a great, endless love the Father has for each one of us that no matter what we've done nor who we were before meeting HIM, we are now called THE CHILDREN OF GOD!

Prayer for the Day

Thank you, Lord God Almighty, for calling us unto Yourself and giving us NEW LIFE and a new family! Amen!

The Father's Love

*"Behold, what manner of **love the Father hath bestowed upon us**, that we should be called the sons of God: therefore the world knoweth us not, because it knew him not."*
I John 3:1 (KJV)

Do you ever feel like a stranger in the world where you walk - in your work, in your home, in the doctor's office, in the grocery store, etc.? Sometimes I look around and wonder, "Why do these folks not KNOW WHOSE THEY ARE?" Then, I realize it is up to me to share the **love of God** with them.

Just last week I was in line at Wal-Mart when a young Mexican Mama was having difficulty with her order. She had a small baby with her. I spoke to her in Spanish, cooed with the baby, and shared a bit with Mama. It was necessary for her to return to the baby aisle for more juice. She asked me if I would watch her baby. Of course, I said "yes" so she hurriedly went for the juice. When she returned, she thanked me over and over.

The clerk at the register said, "That is strange that she trusted you." My thought was "She sensed the love of God in me and knew I wouldn't hurt her child." It was an opportunity to minister to the Mama, the clerk and the manager in charge as I shared a bit about our Mexico Mission to Piedras Negras, Mexico. That's what we have to share with our world - the **LOVE OF THE FATHER!**

Prayer for the Day

*Lord, help us each to be available to those around us so **YOUR LOVE** can overcome the fear, hate, and judgment of the world where we walk. Amen!*

The Father's Love 2: The Father's Caring Heart

"This is My commandment, that you love one another [just] as I have loved you."
John 15:12 (AMP)

As we meditate upon the love of the Father being poured out upon the earth, we are reminded that Jesus said to love our neighbor as we love ourselves and as He loved us. (Matt. 5:43; 19:19; John 15:12) Wow! The love of Father through Jesus Christ was so strong and pure. He gave HIMSELF for us!

What I have discovered the only way to love as He did is to allow His life to be alive and well in me each day. I make that choice early each morning as I awaken, choosing His love and care over my day and asking Him to use me to be a light everywhere I go.

One day this past week I felt a nudge to go to the store in the middle of the day. I didn't want to go; I had wanted to stay home all day. However, the thought became stronger and stronger, so I drove to the store and as I checked out, I glanced over to see a woman I hadn't seen in a long time sitting on a bench. I went over to greet her, and she held onto me for a long time. I sat beside her and listened as she poured out her heart, telling me her grandson had recently died as well as some other situations in her life. We bowed our heads and prayed together. **The love of God surrounded us right there in that busy place** so that **she was refreshed by His love**. Just as we finished praying, she was called in for her appointment.

God's timing is perfect! We must listen closely to His voice and obey immediately what He is telling us to do to carry HIS LIGHT, HIS LOVE, HIS REFRESHING to a hurting world.

Prayer for the Day

Thank you, Lord Jesus, for Your caring heart toward the people in our community. Help us to hear Your voice distinctly and be messengers of Your love everywhere we go! Amen!

Steadfast Love

*"The steadfast love of the Lord never ceases.
His mercies never come to an end.
They are new every morning; great is thy faithfulness."*
Lam. 3:22-23 (RSV)

We use to sing that song during the 1970's, but I have used it over and over in my life to remind me of the unending, ever-present, free-flowing love of the Most High God. Just think of yourself sitting where the spout of His love is being poured freely upon you. Take a moment and allow that love to bring a refreshing to your life in the midst of the busyness of your day! Bask in HIS LOVE - receive from HIS MERCY - be refreshed in HIS GOODNESS!

I'll never forget the morning after I learned John would have to have open-heart surgery. As I was driving the 30 miles back to the hospital, that song rose in my heart so I raised my voice as loudly as possible to declare the goodness and mercies of God in our lives. Truly, as the years have passed, He has proven His steadfast love and care to us over and over and over again. Enjoy His presence today!

Prayer for the Day

Thank you, Lord God, for Your never-ending, satisfying, rejuvenating, ever-infilling LOVE! Amen!

Joy

"But the fruit of the Spirit is love, joy . . ."

Galatians 5:22

Fruit of Joy

"But the fruit of the Spirit is love, joy…"
Galatians 5:22 (RSV)

As the Lord spoke to the people of Israel to free them from the bondage of four hundred years of slavery, they moved out in masses to reach freedom land. When they made it across the Red Sea, they began to rejoice in the Lord God Almighty. Miriam danced; others joined her as they all gave praise for their freedom.

When Christ came into my heart as my Savior, He dried my tears of remorse and gave me a song in my heart. Even though at that time, my voice wasn't all it should be, He didn't care because He loves the praises of His people. Even though I had always been one who would giggle and have fun, the new life gave me more joy to express because of the cleansing I had received from my Lord. The hymns Granny played began to come alive to me.

He lives! He lives!
Christ Jesus lives today!
He walks with me and talks with
me along life's narrow way.
He lives! He lives! Salvation to impart…
You ask me how I know He lives .
. . He lives within my heart!

*Rejoice! Rejoice, oh, Christian!
Lift up your voice and sing
Glory hallelujah to Jesus Christ the King!
The hope of all who seek Him,
The help of all who find,
None other is so loving, so good and kind!*

With that for a testimony, how can any one of us be anything but joyful?

Prayer for the Day

Thank you, Lord God, for granting me full joy to walk each day! Amen!

Joy

*"I have told you these things that My joy and delight may be in you, and that your joy and gladness may be **full measure** and **complete** and **overflowing**. This is My commandment, that you love one another [just] as I have loved you." (Jesus)*
John 15:11 (AMP)

Years ago I was taught that **JOY** is spelled:

JESUS
OTHERS
YOU

I have learned the only way to remain filled with JOY is to keep my eyes and heart ever upon the SAVIOR and the FULLNESS OF THE FATHER through the power of the Holy Spirit. When I have my mind on myself and the circumstances around me, my joy is robbed. When I think of OTHERS ahead of myself, I am living the example of Christ as He walked the earth. Then, my personal needs are met through fulfilling His purpose for my life. My joy remains full.

Prayer for the Day

Lord God, thank you that Your JOY in me comes from dwelling in Your presence, living the life You have called me to live, and sharing with others Your love. Praise Your Holy Name that my joy can be full and complete in YOU! Amen.

Joy Comes

"Let the peace of Christ keep you in tune with each other, in step with each other. None of this going off and doing your own thing. And cultivate thankfulness. Let the Word of Christ - the Message - have the run of the house. Give it plenty of room in your lives. Instruct and direct one another using good common sense. And sing, sing your hearts out to God! Let every detail in your lives - words, actions, whatever - be done in the name of the Master, Jesus, thanking God the Father every step of the way."
Colossians 3:15-17 (The Message)

When PEACE comes to our lives, the by product has to be JOY, or another might contend it's the other way round. However, during the Christmas season we sing praise and worship music wherever we go, hearing the SOUND of rejoicing around us. The joyful sound of Christmas is "Peace on Earth, good will toward men," and we can sing that same JOY all year long.

I'd like to sing these carols all year! (Many times I just do.) "Joy to the world, the Lord is come." We cry out, "Come, Lord Jesus!" when he is saying to us, "I have come. Enjoy my presence." Turn your eyes upon Jesus to look full in His wonderful face and the things of this earth do indeed grow strangely dim. Hallelujah!

In His presence there is fullness of JOY. In His presence, there is Peace. There is LOVE. There is JESUS, the Lord of our lives! Enjoy being with Him during these days. Sing your heart out in praise and thanksgiving for who he is! He is here - present and full of life. PRAISE HIM!

Prayer for the Day

Thank you, Father, for coming to earth as a man so we could see You clearly and understand more distinctly how very much Your love is worth! We sing praise to You, Father, Son and Holy Spirit! Amen!

Joy in the Light

"O house of Jacob, come, let us walk in the light of the Lord."

Isaiah 2:5 (RSV)

Just the other day, we received a marvelous joy movie via internet. One of the quotes was from Helen Keller, who became both blind and deaf because of a childhood illness. Her statement is bold: "Keep your face to the sunshine and you will not see the shadows." Wow! Coming from a lady who could not see or hear, this message carries great power.

Isaiah exhorts us to walk in the light of the Lord. Helen exhorts us to sense the sunlight in order to ward off the darkness around us. Throughout the scriptures, Jesus is referred to as the light of the world. The night he was born, there was a bright star to mark the place. When God created the world, he said, "Let there be light." I believe with all my heart that when Jesus was born, the light of freedom entered our world to overcome all darkness. When light brings life, joy follows - actually an overwhelming sense of rejoicing!

In every day, we must turn our faces toward the warmth of the light of life in Jesus Christ, and truly the things of this earth will grow strangely dim in the light of his wonder and grace. Enjoy the glory he brought to earth as you seek His face!

Prayer for the Day

Father, may Your light so illumine our hearts that joy overflows in Your presence, pushing out any doubt, fear or unbelief as we celebrate the arrival of Your Son every day to enjoy the light of His resurrection power in our lives! Amen!

Joy Is Strength!

". . . for the joy of the Lord is our strength."
Nehemiah 8:10 (RSV)

We have been centering upon the JOY. Today let's consider the STRENGTH! God told Joshua 3 times in Chapter 1 to "*be strong and very courageous.*" *(AMP)*

As I have contemplated that STRENGTH of God today, I have experienced it coursing through me. I have been really tired from a virus that tried to pull me down. Last night I prayed for the Lord to strengthen me to do all He has on board for me right now. This morning, I claimed His joy to be full and overflowing. As a result I have experienced great strength and have been able to work almost eight hours helping someone else! ☺

What a mighty God we serve! What a **joy** it is to know Him! What **strength** exudes from His presence! Amen!

Enjoy the ride . . . Call upon HIS STRENGTH and JOY! We must have HIM in us to fulfill His call upon us in our everyday life!

Prayer for the Day

Today as we go forth, may His joy fill us in a new way so that we can spill it out on others - even through our cracked cups! Amen!

The Joy of the Lord

". . . and do not be grieved, for the joy of the Lord is your strength."
Nehemiah 8:10 (RSV)

When we are soaring high like the eagle it is easy to enjoy life and the thrill of living. They play in the air, dipping down and then riding the thermal currents without a care in the world. However, if one threatens to come near their nest, they will valiantly rise up and fight for the life of their mate or their offspring.

Many of us find it easy to have joy when everything is going well, but it's in the hard places that JOY must be a CHOICE. When we see ourselves taking hold of the bad news or see those around us suffering, we have to set our vision on the SON and allow HIM to be our JOY and our SALVATION!

In the old chorus we used to sing, "The Joy of the Lord Is My Strength," we added a verse where we Ha, Ha, Ha, Ha'd through it all the way. By the time we complete the chorus, the laughter bubbled up inside of us and the JOY of the LORD increases our strength.

Prayer for the Day

Thank you, Father, for giving us laughter in the midst of the world today. Thank YOU we can choose JOY over pain, bad news, sickness, and suffering, for YOU are more than able to lift us high above as we keep our eyes upon YOU! Amen.

Love One Another with Joy

I'm singing "Friend of a Wounded Heart" by Wayne Watson!

> ***Joy**, comes like the morning*
> ***Hope**, deepens as you grow*
> *And peace, beyond the reaches of your soul,*
> *Comes blowing through you, for*
> *love has made you whole.*

Joy is birthed from the presence of God within us. Think about the day you received Him as your Savior and then of the day He became LORD OF YOUR LIFE! JOY comes through His presence in our lives. If you've sprung a leak along the way, breathe out the cause of that leak and refill with HIS PRESENCE! ☺ HIS JOY returns with His presence and our giving Him the position of being LORD OF OUR LIVES!

I call this spiritual breathing - breathe out the doubt, fear, hurt, unbelief, wound, and breathe in His PRESENCE to see Him glorified with joy unspeakable within us!

Prayer for the Day

Thank you, Lord, that as we come together as the Body of Christ, Your joy will be expounded as we join our faith together to prepare to serve You with our whole heart! Amen!

Joy from Salvation

"With joy you will draw water from the wells of salvation."
Isaiah 12:3 (RSV)

Truly the watering of our souls comes from dwelling where the spout of the Lord's love, joy, and strength is poured out for us. Each day as we begin our time with Him privately, we are drawing from the well of salvation. Our initial salvation experience brings us fullness of joy, but to continue to walk in that joy, we have to draw from His water.

How do we do that? We read His written Word; we pray without ceasing, giving thanks to the Lord for He is good; we sing songs of praise; and we continually look to him throughout the day to keep our focus centered upon Him and His purpose for our lives. If all we drank each day was the sip of water we have after we brush our teeth, we would dehydrate in no time. Our spiritual life depends on the water from the living well of salvation – His holy presence alive and well within us. When you're in the car, walking down the street, or working at your job – pause to thank the Lord during the day to refill your well.

The first year I taught in public school, I learned to draw away in the midst of the crowd to rekindle my joy and rejuvenate the Spirit of the Lord within me during the day. Turning my thoughts to Him in the midst of the busyness of the day gave me the added strength I needed to go on. Pausing to think of Him in the midst of dealing with challenging students, new direction would come for helping each one.

Pause and calmly think of Him!

Prayer for the Day

Father, thank you for the watering places open to us. Help us have the discipline to draw from those places regularly. Amen!

More Joy

"Thou hast put more joy in my heart than they have when their grain and wine abound."
Psalms 4:7 (RSV)

When we truly come into the presence of the Living God, we are given the ability to experience pure joy at a brand new high. Some people think happiness is a state of mind or a state of having things, but the joy of the Lord is a fountain coming forth from our innermost being once we grasp was love the Father has for each of us. By spending time in His Word, in prayer, and in communion with Him, we find a joy like no other.

Many know the joy of holding the first child in your arms for the very first time. Suddenly we are so overwhelmed with love for that special one who was birthed out of love between the husband and wife. I'll never forget the first time I held our Ginger in my arms. She was born with fluid on her lungs so she had to be kept in a special nursery for the first 24 hours of her life. When the doctor felt it was safe for her to leave the controlled breathing, she was laid in my arms for the first time. Tears filled my eyes and a love sprang forth from my soul I had never experienced before – the love of a parent for a child. Suddenly I understood how my parents loved me, but more importantly I began to receive revelation of how much Father loves me.

As I spent time with the Lord, His love for me became more and more evident. The more time I stayed in His presence, the more joy bubbled forth from my own spirit. What an amazing love He has given to us – to take us right where we are and hold us close to His heart so that we can experience more joy than we have ever imagined!

Prayer for the Day

Thank you, Father God, for holding me so close to Your heart that pure joy overflows from mine. Amen!

Sing for Joy

"For thou, O Lord, hast made me glad by thy work; at the works of thy hands I sing for joy."
Psalms 92:4 (RSV)

God Himself has made me glad by allowing me to experience His love in creation as well as His tender mercies each day. He has taught me to enter His presence with thanksgiving in my heart and to enter His courts with praise. When I thank Him for all He has done in my life or begin to praise Him for all He has done to be certain my life would be complete and fulfilled, I cannot help but sing His songs of joy.

Teaching in a public high school, I was able to sponsor a prayer group along with a close colleague for twenty-eight years. We met with students and teachers before school began each day. During the week the students would lead devotions for the group, but on Friday we sang scripture choruses as well as other songs of praise. What a glorious way to begin every Friday morning. By the time we finished our singing and had prayer together, my strength was renewed like the eagles so tiredness of the week was no longer a concern. I could walk into the corridors with a song in my heart, a spring in my step, and a smile on my face.

One day a student came to my door to talk with me. Her remark was "I've been watching you, Mrs. Russell. I want to know what makes you so happy all the time.

What gives you so much to smile about?" Well, that was a marvelous opportunity. She and I shared after school hours how the Lord had changed my life and turned me from a complainer to a singer. Of course, she wanted to know how to have that same experience and prayed right there to receive Christ as her Savior. Through the years she has grown in her faith. God has used her to bring joy to others.

Prayer for the Day

Thank you, Lord, for making joy such a gift in our lives. Help us to sing our way through to victory each day so we can be a blessing to others to draw them into Your kingdom! Amen!

Refreshment of Joy

"For I have derived much joy and comfort from your love, my brother, because the hearts of your saints have been refreshed through you."
Philemon 7 (RSV)

Paul shares his love for Philemon in the opening verses of this short epistle. He commends him for being refreshment to the people around him expressing his own joy at seeing him used of the Lord in a mighty way. Sharing this joy with Philemon encouraged him to continue spreading that joy to others as he ministered to them. When we are in need of a refreshing, sometimes we need fellow believers to come around us to share the great things God is doing in their lives. Other times we just need someone to come along to bring a smile, a laugh, a good story, or just a pat on the back.

When others encourage us, we are motivated to reach out a helping hand to others. Many times in public education, young people came to school with heavy hearts – disagreement between parents, divorce, mistreatment at home, rejection from friends, afraid of the future and weary of the present. As a classroom teacher, I could give a smile, a note on a paper of encouragement, a listening ear when one was needed, or a fun song in the classroom that lifted everyone's attitude for the day. Many of my students told me how they looked forward to coming into the room because they never knew what fun was planned for the day. Don't misunderstand me – I expected a great deal from my students; however, learning can be filled with fun, laughter and goodness. After all laughter brings health to your bones as it refreshes your entire being.

We must share a little joy along the way of life. Take it in from the Father, give it out to everyone you see, and watch your world become a more joyful place!

Prayer for the Day

Father, make me an instrument of your joy! Let me share laughter, love, and encouragement with everyone I see! Amen!

Peace

"But the fruit of the Spirit is love, joy, peace . . ."

Galatians 5:22

Peace as Fruit

*"But the fruit of the Spirit is love, joy, **peace . . .**"*
Galatians 5:22-23 (RSV)

The Greek word for *peace* is *eirene*, which means "wholeness, completeness, or tranquility in the soul that is unaffected by the outward circumstances or pressures" according to one definition. Actually it intimates rule of order coming in the midst of chaos. Isn't it interesting that we easily talk about joy as a fruit of the Spirit, or kindness, love, faithfulness, etc. But how many times to we worry and fret, not cashing in on the **FRUIT OF PEACE**?

When we walk in **peace,** love and joy exude from us. When we dwell in the safety of the Most High God, we are able to maintain our **peace** in the midst of diverse circumstances. Our **peace** is not dependent on circumstances or on what others may do. It is a choice within us to walk in the fruit of God's Holy Spirit in our lives.

Peace came to earth over 2000 years ago in the form of Jesus Christ. Why do we struggle to try to help God solve the solutions around us when He has already made a way and paid the price for our **peace**?

Prayer for the Day

*Lord God, today I choose to walk in Your **peace** - the peace that only the Holy Spirit within me can bring. I receive Your power in a fresh new way to be at peace with myself because You paved the way for my serenity to be real in every single day. Forgive me when I've tried to do it myself. Fill me with your Holy Presence so that Your Holy Peace can be in me as a great example of Your love! Amen!*

Peace

*"But the fruit of the Spirit is love, joy, **peace** . . ."*
Galatians 5:22-23 (RSV)

One of the definitions for **peace** in the Merriam-Webster Dictionary is "*a state of calm or quiet*"; another is "*freedom from disturbing thoughts or emotions.*"

Many of us deal with disturbing thoughts and emotions because of the busy-ness of the day, the stress of our lives, and the insecurities we often feel in relationships with others. In Colossians 3:15 we are exhorted to ". . . *let the **peace** of Christ rule in your hearts, to which indeed you were called in the one body. And be thankful.*"

I have discovered that when the disturbing thoughts come I must

TURN MY EYES UPON JESUS
LOOK FULL IN HIS WONDERFUL FACE
AND THE THINGS OF EARTH WILL
GROW STRANGELY DIM
IN THE LIGHT OF HIS GLORY AND GRACE!

In I Corinthians 10:13 we read "*No temptation has overtaken you that is not common to man. God is FAITHFUL, and he will not let you be tempted beyond your strength, but with the temptation will also provide the way of escape, that you may be able to endure it.*" Many years ago, the Lord spoke to my heart "the way of escape is through praise." So, when I am anxious, I call upon His name and give Him praise for His **peace** in the midst of any and all circumstances.

Prayer for the Day

*Thank you, Father, for providing for my **PEACE** in the midst of my daily challenges. You are greater than anything else in all creation. I claim your **renewed peace** for THIS DAY! Glory to your holy, righteous NAME! Amen.*

Shalom

"Then Gideon perceived that he was the angel of the Lord; and Gideon said, 'Alas, O Lord God! For now I have seen the angel of the Lord face to face.' But the Lord said to him, 'Peace be to you; do not fear, you shall not die.' Then Gideon built an altar there to the Lord, and called it, called it Jehovahshalom . . ."
Judges 6:22-24 (KJV)

Jehovah Shalom means literally "the Lord is peace" as was quoted in the above scripture. S*halom* is translated *peace* 170 times. The definition according to the Hebrew meanings could be "whole," "finished," "fulfilled," "well," or "welfare." Shalom is the kind of peace that results from being a whole person in right relationship to God and to one's fellow man.

However, most of us think of **peace** as being a state of life without any conflict. However, the real meaning of *shalom* is to be at peace in the midst of conflict. When we say to pray for the peace of Jerusalem (that is part of it), we are asking that Jerusalem be "complete" and "whole."

Our **peace** is not dependent upon others; it is totally a choice for our lives. In the midst of the last few weeks, we can have **peace** within ourselves even though others may reject us, our finances may not be secure, or unrest is around us. **Peace** is the result of resting in a relationship with God and comes from seeking Him in our daily lives. The peace of God that passes all understanding can be ours throughout each day!

Prayer for the Day

*Father, today I choose peace in my own life! I appropriate Your power in my life to maintain **peace** for this day. As my day unfolds, may I remind myself that You are JEHOVAH SHALOM - more than sufficient to bring me **peace** in every moment of my life! Amen!*

God's Peace

"And God's peace [shall be yours, that tranquil state of a soul assured of its salvation through Christ, and so fearing nothing from God and being content with its earthly lot of whatever sort that is, that peace] which transcends all understanding shall garrison and mount guard over your hearts and minds in Christ Jesus."
Philippians 4:7 (AMP)

Many of us can quote the above scripture; however, we move through our day being concerned about things that are totally out of our control. For example, when my grandmother died of cancer in 1963, I began to deal with a fear of cancer. Her death was slow, painful, and would cause her to moan out loud. Sleeping in the room above hers, I could hear her throughout the night. What a great relief her passing was for her body. However, for me it began a journey to walk away from fear.

In 1970 after being filled with the Holy Spirit, the Lord began to work in my life to set me free at many levels. At that time I didn't realize the fear of cancer, but as my body began to manifest several problems with cysts, tumors, etc., I knew help was needed. I would deny the fear of cancer; I would refute it and cast it out; and I would declare it had no right to me. But it wasn't until I was in worship in a CBU Conference at Ridgecrest, NC, in the early 1980's that I was totally set free from the fear of cancer. It was as if God placed his arms around my shoulders and whispered in my ear, "You do not have to fear. I am your God. Nothing is too hard for me." As we continued to worship, this great peace came over me that literally passes all understanding to keep my heart and mind on HIM in the midst of battles that came.

Dad had died with cancer in 1980. Mom was diagnosed with breast cancer in 1990 and had two mastectomies one right after the other. I had a suspicious breast biopsy in 1992. Each time the word *cancer* was mentioned, the great **peace** came over me after my encounter in North Carolina. Before that, it would send me reeling. Just this past Christmas, I had another suspicious mammogram. When a friend called with the news, she had already set up my next session. Over that weekend, the peace of God flooded my heart. Truly I had NO FEAR - only HIS CONFIDENT ASSURANCE that He is more than enough.

The tests were clear! Glory to God for His peace no matter what the circumstances!

Prayer for the Day

Father, as we walk away from fear, we choose to walk toward your peace. Thank you for guarding our hearts with Your power and peace that transcends all understanding. Thank you for Your great and mighty peace that truly passes all understanding. Amen!

Peace on Earth

"Glory to God in the highest, and on earth **peace***, good will among men with whom he is pleased!"*

Luke 2:14 (RSV)

During our most recent Bible Study, our final lesson was "To Know Him through Peace." While I was teaching the last day, the Lord brought me to a fresh, renewed understanding of His great and mighty **peace.** Through the years we have known **peace** in many circumstances, we have studied **peace** as a fruit of the Holy Spirit, we have prayed for **peace** for our world, and we have declared **peace** over our home. However, I SAW in my heart of hearts Jesus coming to earth.

We know Jesus manifested LOVE, FORGIVENESS, FULFILLMENT, JOY, GRACE, and LIFE. We know His great **PEACE** was prophesied in the Old Testament in Jehovah Shalom (Our God is peace). But I want you to envision the precious baby arriving in Bethlehem, lying in the manger with the star shining brightly over head.

PEACE came to earth that night! **JESUS is PEACE**, the personified Father on the face of the earth. **PEACE** in an earthen vessel to bring glad tidings of great joy and good will to all men. **Peace** to share HIS LIFE with all who would receive HIM. **PEACE ON EARTH, GOOD WILL TO ALL!**

The greatest news of all is that He will come again!

Prayer for the Day

As we go about our day, we ask You, Lord God Almighty, to make us so aware that YOUR GREAT PEACE dwells within us through Your Son. God, help us to be PEACE on earth, good will to all men, as we live in the rest of knowing we are Your children on earth! Amen!

Blessing of the Lord

"The Lord bless thee, and keep thee: The Lord make his face shine upon thee, and be gracious unto thee; The Lord lift up his countenance upon thee, and give thee peace."
Numbers 6:24-26 (KJV)

These were the instructions to Aaron and his sons from the Lord God. The fathers of Hebrew households have used this blessing over their families for generations. When we were taken into the family of God through his precious Son Jesus Christ, we too were given right to this magnanimous blessing. Each night as our children put their children to bed, they recite this blessing over them. When our children were young, we blessed them each night with "Jesus loves you. Daddy loves you. Mama loves you, etc." As our grandchildren came along, we began the same blessing any time they spent the night with us, using their mamas and daddies and other grandparents as well. They are truly a loved bunch!

As I ponder each day, our prayer for you would be Numbers 6. May you be blessed coming in and going out! May you have the peace of God along your way! May you find the face of God in all you do, and may His light so shine in your life that His everlasting love, joy and peace will resound around your every move. You see, just as the Hebrew people were blessed, so are we Christians with the promise of Jesus Christ: *"Peace I leave with you, my peace I give unto you: not as the world giveth, give I unto you. Let not your heart be troubled, neither let it be afraid."* **John 14:27**

Prayer for the Day

Thank you, Father, for Your gift of peace! Thank you for Your complete love and joy! Praise Your holy name for granting us the privilege of walking in Your light so our path will be brighter and brighter each day! Amen!

Perfect Peace

*"Thou dost keep him in perfect peace,
whose mind is stayed on thee,
because he trusts in thee."*

Isaiah 26:3 (RSV)

When the storms of life hit, I remind myself that Jesus spoke to the storm to say, "Peace! Be still!" and the wind ceased. Life often offers us specific challenges where we try our best to figure out the solution to the problem rather than wait in the presence of God for the peace to come to us. True peace is not when everything is going great. True peace is walking in victory in the midst of great difficulty because we know Whose we are so we are persuaded that nothing can separate us from the love of God in Christ Jesus.

How would one describe perfect peace? - Sitting by the shore watching the waves hit the beach? Sitting in a boat in the middle of a serene lake? Camping on the high mountains by a stream? Standing in corporate worship service singing high praise? Resting in the cool of the evening under a shade tree while watching a hummingbird fly around? Standing on snow-capped mountains as close to the sky as possible? Everyone has their own peaceful resting place.

Mine is in the presence of Father God – whether I'm at the ocean, lake, mountain, island, or in the midst of a life-threatening crisis in a hospital. The place of peace goes everywhere I do because Jesus Christ lives inside of me as my Lord and Savior, the Holy Spirit guides my steps, and Father surrounds me with His love.

Whatever difficult place you may find yourself today, give God an opportunity to give you peace for your soul. Tell Him you trust in Him. Give Him the problem and leave it at His throne. He is more than able to take care of anything, any time, anywhere. He is the PEACEFUL CARETAKER!

Prayer for the Day

Thank you, Lord God, for giving me peace in the midst of this day! Amen!

Return of the Redeemed

*"For you shall go our in joy, and be led forth
in peace; the mountains and the hills before
you shall break forth into singing, and all the
trees of the field shall clap their hands."*
Isaiah 55:12 (RSV)

When we enter into the presence of God to find His rest in the midst of the storm, we find strength in His perfect peace. He gives us the refreshing that breaks out in songs of joy. Did you know where there is praise and worship to the King of Kings, no enemy can stand in the midst of that place? When the Lord promised us that no temptation would overcome us but that He would grant us a way of escape, that way He gave us was worship!

The redeemed, those of us who know Christ as our Savior, will go forth with joy and be led by peace! Wow! In today's world that sounds impossible but with God nothing is impossible. It is our choice whether we live in peace or be upset by the trivial things in each day. It is our choice whether the storms of life control us or we are in the control of God Almighty. Our choice must be to rest in the arms of Father God, learn to gain strength there, and go forth with singing into each day with victory on our minds.

There is no room for depression, sadness, disappointment, fear or doubt in the presence of God Almighty. Draw close to Him and He will be as close as your next breath! Make a decision to walk in the victory of the Lord Jesus Christ, resurrected from the dead, breathing life into our very souls! We have a song to sing!

Prayer for the Day

Thank you for granting me the privilege of going out with joy and being led forth with peace! Amen!

Patience

"But the fruit of the Spirit is love, joy, peace, patience..."

Galatians 5:22

Fruit of Patience

"But the fruit of the Spirit is love, joy, peace, patience..."
Galatians 5:22 (RSV)

We had been visiting various churches in 1970 to find a new home church where we could attend as a family. A friend from work invited us to his church so we went to Sunday School with him and his wife before attending service that morning. The following Wednesday morning, the Sunday School teacher showed up at our door to visit!

Shirley was a marvelous person who truly cared about each of the people visiting her class. As we talked in our living room with our two girls under the age of two running and playing in the next room, she asked if I were a Christian and "What is the greatest need in your life?" Well, I didn't hesitate, "Patience! When I taught school, I had no problem with patience because the children came and went, but now mine are here 24/7 so there is a need for endurance with patience all the time."

We laughed together because Shirley also had small children at home. Then she shared with me about the infilling of the Holy Spirit who came to bring us the power to live life to the fullest after Jesus Christ ascended into heaven. She said the Holy Spirit is a gift from Father God to help us, teach us, and guide us along the way. As we talked about various scriptures, my mind was opened to understand why I had such need in my life.

After thinking about the teaching for several days and reading the scripture references she left me from Acts 1-2 and John 14:26, one afternoon just after the girls had gone down for their naps, I sat down at the dining room table to write God a letter. I listed everything that had blocked His power in my life; then I prayed to be filled with the Holy Spirit. There were no lightning bolts, but there was a great peace that came over my life as well as great insight into the Word of God. Thus, the fruit of patience began to grow within me as I practiced God's teaching.

Prayer for the Day

Father, forgive me of all my sin. Wash me clean again. Come into my life in the fullness of the Holy Spirit to complete Your purpose for my life. Amen!

Patience

"For you have need of steadfast patience and endurance, so that you may perform and fully accomplish the will of God, and thus receive and carry away [and enjoy to the full] what is promised.
Hebrews 10:36 (AMP)

You may say, "Oh, my, I don't want to talk about patience right now. I've waited long enough. I want God to move NOW!"

As we grow in the fruit of the Holy Spirit, all of us have experienced impatience while waiting on God or on people! Many have said, "Don't pray for patience because you'll be trained to wait." However, what we must do is appropriate patience in every situation we encounter.

When we moved to Tennessee in 1974, we were so excited because God had called us to this region. We had vision of what He wanted us to do, so we wanted it accomplished right then! However, our experience has been "little by little" we possess the land given into our hands, including the land within us.

Hebrews 10:36 remained on our refrigerator for years. We would read it, claim in, stand on it, refuse to give in to doubts that ravaged our minds, etc. Finally, revelation came: "Patience is a fruit of the Spirit." God has already given it to us. We must claim it for ourselves.

Prayer for the Day

Father, help us to walk in Your patience. Fill us with Your goodness and grace that we might appropriate this fruit every day in every circumstance. Amen!

Patience in Circumstances

"For you have need of steadfast patience and endurance, so that you may perform and fully accomplish the will of God, and thus receive and carry away [and enjoy to the full] what is promised."

Hebrews 10:36 (AMP)

As we are discussing *patience*, I thought you'd enjoy Webster's definition: "the capacity, habit or fact of being patient." The definition for *patient* is "bearing pain or trials without complaint; showing self-control; calm; steadfast; persevering." Now it's one thing to be patient with your children or your boss, but it's quite another to bear pain or trials without complaint.

According to Unger's Bible Dictionary, there are two Greek words for patience: one having to do with endurance, constancy, forbearance, and long-suffering; the other referring to steadfastness, constancy, a patient waiting for. Both of these together are summed up by stating: "Patience is that calm and unruffled temper with which the good man bears the evils of life, whether they proceed from persons or things."

Now, having unruffled tempers in the midst of uncontrollable circumstances is a pretty tall order. However, when we consider Jesus and His endurance as he faced the accusers over and over throughout his ministry, we can know for a fact that patience is possible. We can also learn from what He did.

Jesus drew away from the crowds, sought the face of Father, and rested in His presence. We too must pull away in the midst of agitating circumstances, accusations, and ruffled feathers to renew the "right spirit within us."

Prayer for the Day

Lord God, right now I commit my heart and mind to You in the midst of the trials of life. I appropriate Your peace, Your rest and Your patience for this moment of my life. Amen!

Patience in Action

"So don't throw it all away now. You were sure of yourselves then. It's still a sure thing! But you need to stick it out, staying with God's plan so you'll be there for the promised completion."
Hebrews 10:35-36 (The Message)

When I was hired to teach English at David Crockett High School in the 1970's, I had great dreams of helping young people in many facets of life. Being floored by the pessimism I witnessed in many leaders, I wanted to run through halls, praying to bring down strongholds, and releasing the presence of God everywhere. I wanted to paint "Be Positive!" signs throughout the building and see immediate response to optimism. However, as the weeks passed, I began to realize Rome definitely wasn't built in a day.

Becoming discouraged, I sought the Lord as well as a prayer partner to agree for God's power to be released in a great way. My prayer partner suggested I pull away during the day when I could and pray for refreshing in order to combat the discouragement. So, I did just that - between classes, during my lunch time, before and after school time. Through the years, the great habit of drawing into His presence kept me safe and secure. In many instances, I would devote my entire lunch time to prayer and resting in Him rather than spending time with others. His strength became stronger; his purposes became clearer; my vision clarified; and my resolve to follow through became stronger than my desire to throw in the towel.

After twenty-eight years in the same school, my testimony is God did great things through touching the lives of many people, both students and adults. In the process, He changed me and taught me great patience in many different circumstances. I didn't always pass the test, but I was always given another opportunity to learn. He's still working on me!

Prayer for the Day

Thank you, Father, for never giving up on my inabilities. Praise Your Holy Righteous Name for granting me Your divine patience to replace my human frailty over and over again. Today, I appropriate Your patience in my life to walk with Your light shining through me! Amen!

Bring Forth Fruit

"And as for that in the good soil, they are those who, hearing the word, hold it fast in an honest and good heart, and bring forth fruit with patience."
Luke 8:13 (RSV)

Jesus explains the parable of the sower in Luke 8:9-18 after His disciples asked what the story meant which He had just shared. As He talks along the way, He teaches there are good soil, rocky soil, as well as thorny ground. Finishing the summary, we see clearly that fruit is brought forth with much patience.

We know seed planted today won't come up immediately, yet we want everything instantly. However, if our lives are good soil – lives that are nurtured in the Word of God, spending time in prayer, and meditating on the teachings of the Lord God. We have to put the Word in, water the Word through understanding, and practice the Word in order for the fruit to come forth. As one season flows into the next, we shall see the fruit produced by the goodness of God dwelling in us.

Practice, practice, practice seems to be the secret to living a life filled with love, joy, peace, and patience. We have time. Let's get started practicing today.

Prayer for the Day

Father, help me be diligent in studying Your Word, in practicing Your teaching, and in spending time in prayer with You each day. Amen!

Establish Your Heart

"You also be patient. Establish your hearts, for the coming of the Lord is at hand."
James 5:8 (RSV)

How many times are we in a doctor's office, sitting, waiting, looking at our watches and wondering "How much longer is this going to take?" We certainly are an impatient lot of people, always in a hurry, always thinking about what we have to do next. We find it difficult to enjoy the moment for thinking about the next day, next week or next year. We seem to be moving ahead at such a pace that if the Lord should return, one wonders if we might miss it because we are so caught up in the world.

Of course, that will not happen. When Jesus comes to get His own, He'll have no problem recognizing the ones who have spent time with Him! He'll know exactly who is who. However, in the meantime, why don't we learn to enjoy the moment by establishing our hearts to think about God and His Word instead of worrying about the little details of the day? God can take care of all the details when we give them to Him. He'll do much better than we can even think as we set our eyes upon Him to not lose our cool in the midst of trying circumstances.

Learning to set our minds on Christ Jesus helps us to establish our hearts for the purpose of the Kingdom in each moment we are alive. Instead of becoming impatient, ask the Lord if there is anyone sitting in that waiting room that might need someone to talk to or someone to just smile at them. We can be used wherever we are to bring a blessing to those around us. We must be patient, establish our hearts in the Word, and keep our vision on the one who has called us to be His set-apart-ones.

Prayer for the Day

Father, help me keep my mind upon You as I go through this day. Help me to turn my eyes upon You so the little things of this earth will grow strangely dim in the light of Your wonder and grace. Amen!

Be Patient in Tribulation

"Rejoice in your hope, be patient in tribulation, be constant in prayer."
Romans 12:12 (RSV)

In recent years our family has had one medical situation after another which has given us many hours in the waiting rooms of doctors' offices throughout our region as well as in New York, Georgia, and other places. In the beginning of the medical onslaught, it was difficult for me to sit and to wait. It always seemed no matter what time the appointment, there was always sitting in the waiting room, then sitting in the doctor's office, followed by waiting for blood work and the test results to return so decisions could be made. Then there came the time of waiting for the right place, the right doctor, and the right time for the answer to be revealed. Waiting, waiting, waiting, waiting, waiting and on it goes.

Now after years of practice and turning my thoughts on Christ Jesus in various situations where we've had to wait, I have learned I'm usually there for a Kingdom purpose, whether the appointment is for myself or one of my family members. As I look around the place where we are, there is always someone in need of comfort, a listening ear, or just a smile that comes from the heart of God. The Lord has used this time to allow us to minister to a hurting world – one that is full of pain without the marvelous answer of God's endless love flowing to them. Often He gives me the privilege of sharing His love with another while waiting to receive my own family's answer. In that way truly I have learned patience in tribulation.

Truly there is no sickness, distress, peril or trial that can separate us from the love of God in Christ Jesus. Rejoice in our hope, practice patience in tribulation and remain in prayer for the strength to complete each assignment with joy!

Prayer for the Day

Open our eyes, Lord, to the hurting world around us as You care for the concerns in our own lives. Help us to be instruments of peace in a world filled with turmoil and pain. Amen!

Love Is Patient

"Love is patient and kind..."
I Corinthians 13:4 (RSV)

To say the Lord Jesus Christ was patient is definitely an understatement. Even though He knew what was ahead in His life, He was willing to give His all that we might have life more abundantly. (John 10:10) He was also kind to all He met. Being patient is the inherent nature of God Almighty because He has shown us His great promises and has waited for us to come to Him.

In the late 1990's my husband and I were privileged to visit Israel. John had open-heart surgery one year and the next we found ourselves with provision to travel to the Holy Land! During the visits to the places where Jesus walked as well as learning about the historical places of the Old Testament, we were traveling in large groups. As the women stood in line to use the restroom, we chatted, shared our life stories, and discussed things we were seeing. As we waited in different restaurants to be served, we were able to become acquainted with many folks from all over the world. When visiting different places, we had to report to the bus on time so as not to waste time for others.

About the third day out, our tour leader began a little chorus that I have now sung for many years:

Patience, patience, patience,
Just a little bit of patience.
Joy, joy, joy,
Just a little bit of joy.

We continued to sing that song over and over and over again during the ten-day journey. What was so marvelous about the song was we could sing it anywhere we were waiting, for any occasion, and for release of tension that might grow in a group of 350 people. I've used it many times since that trip to center my vision on Christ Jesus and appropriate His patience through the Holy Spirit to gain control of emotions, weariness, and various circumstances in life.

Prayer for the Day

Thank you, Lord God, that You always make a way of escape for us in difficult situations. Help us to remain calm, cool, and collected with Your great patience! Amen!

Kindness

"But the fruit of the Spirit is love, joy, peace, patience, kindness..."

Galatians 5:22

Kindness

*"But the fruit of the Spirit is love, joy, peace, patience, **kindness**..."*
Galatians 5:22 (RSV)

As we have discussed the fruit of the Spirit, we move from love to joy to peace to patience and now to *kindness*. According to Webster, *kind* is to be of "a sympathetic, forbearing, or pleasant nature, or arising from sympathy or forbearance." According to Unger's Bible Dictionary, *kindness* is "having zeal toward another in a good sense." Kindness springs from the Hebrew word *hĕsĕd,* which deals with God's goodness, mercy, benefits, etc.

The loving kindness of the Lord God was poured out for all mankind when He sent Jesus Christ to the earth to become our replacement as he died on the cross. Think about that much "loving kindness"! Oh, my, it's hard to fathom the depth, height, width, breadth of His love for us! ***Kindness** is overflowing in our lives because of that love.*

Many people think of God's wrath, but we must center in on His great *kindness*. We must appropriate His *kind* words and deeds in order to experience the full grace of His love toward us. How many of us would like to receive great *kindness* from others? It has been my experience that as I am *kind,* others are *kind* toward me . . .

Prayer for the Day

*Father, grant me the patience to use **kindness in my words, my actions, and my deeds**! May this fruit become mature in my everyday life! Amen!*

Words of Kindness

". . . for you have tasted the kindness of the Lord."
I Peter 2:3 (RSV)

Kindness is a gift to everyone who receives it. John's brother, Jackie, graduated into heaven recently. One person said of him, "He was always kind to me." That is an interesting statement because Jackie was always kind in school, in the community and to the people close to him. However, he too could be ruffled in some situations. If he was asked a question, he always responded very politely. What a tribute to a life! He was **KIND**. His gentleness came through his giving nature - to his parents, to his siblings, and to his own daughter. Kindness and gentleness often go hand-in-hand.

When we have tasted of salvation, we experience the sweet kindness of the Lord in our lives. Even when things don't come together like we think, we can remember the day the presence of God entered our lives to know His kindness toward us when we didn't deserve it. Jackie tasted the kindness of the Lord when he received Christ as his Savior. His gentle nature extended that kindness to others. During his illness, he was always kind and appreciative to his doctors, to his family and to his friends. He walked in kindness even when he didn't feel well. Thank you, Lord, Your kindness can be expressed through each of us as we appropriate your love for others.

Prayer for the Day

*Lord, may my words be **kind**. May I never forget that I've tasted Your **kindness** in my life! Thank you for Your gentle nature. Help me be gentle to others. Amen!*

Kindness in Forgiveness

"And he (Joseph) kissed all his brothers and wept upon them; and after that his brothers talked with him."
Genesis 45:15 (RSV)

Most of us are familiar with the Genesis story of Joseph who was sold into slavery and declared dead by his brothers. We remember he spent years as a slave, then as a prisoner, before he was placed in the position of second-highest command in Egypt. Because of God's hand upon Joseph's life, He protected him so the Israelites could be saved in famine.

Amazingly, Joseph was strong, vibrant, obedient, and kind in all his dealings - so much so in fact that he rose to a leadership position everywhere he went. However, the greatest evidence of his kindness was in the forgiveness he showered upon his brothers when they came to Egypt to obtain food during the famine. At first, one believes he is being hard on them because he kept one of the brothers, but that was his guarantee they would return.

How he kept from falling upon them immediately to identify himself is beyond our understanding! God had his hand on Joseph. He had learned to forgive; he could recognize God's destiny; and he was willing to do whatever he had to do to fulfill God's purpose for his life. When he identified himself to his brothers, he gave them the greatest gift – forgiveness – to replace their fear of what he might do!

Is there anyone you haven't forgiven? Take a moment right now to hold that person to the Lord God and ask for His mercy upon his life.

Prayer for the Day

Lord God, thank you for granting me the ability to forgive any wrong done to me in this world. Give me the kindness of loving my fellowman and receiving him in every situation. Thank you for that privilege. Amen.

Kindness of the Heart

"On the third day Joseph said to them, "Do this and you will live, for I fear God: . . .and bring your youngest brother to me so your words will be verified . . ."
Genesis 42:18-20 (RSV)

As I have pondered Joseph's kindness over the past few days, I continue to be overwhelmed by his action of kissing his brothers and weeping upon them. Remember, they sold him into slavery; they lied to their father; they lived any old way they pleased during the years he was in slavery and in prison. However, when he saw them face to face the very first time, he was moved with COMPASSION. Even though he gave them a difficult time, it was because he wanted to be reunited with his father and brother.

His brothers didn't recognize him because they would never have expected him to be a ruler. Also, they were in great need and were unsure they would be accepted in Egypt. Considering their own fears, they were moved by their emotions, not by reality around them.

Joseph, on the other hand, was seeing his dreams come true. Now he could be restored to his family . . . He could help them instead of harming them. He had great decisions to make. Jesus told his disciples to "turn the other cheek."

Joseph didn't have the Holy Spirit; he didn't know Jesus; but He knew Father God. He trusted HIM, forgave his brothers, and as a result was reunited with all his family! What a heart!

Prayer for the Day

Father, please grant me the same heart to forgive those who have wronged me! Give me a heart of love and forgiveness so that Your Kingdom may be enhanced by love and kindness! Amen!

The Kindness of the Lord

"And Lot said to them (the angels), Oh, no, my lords; behold, your servant has found favor in your sight, and you have shown me great kindness in saving my life . . ."
Genesis 19:18-19 (RSV)

We remember the story of the destruction of Sodom and Gomorrah. Lot and his family were given life for leaving the evil city behind. Lot's wife looked back and was turned to a pillar of salt. Lot told the angels he had experienced "kindness" because his life was saved by leaving the city. (Genesis 19:15-26)

We too have experienced salvation from death because of the deliverance of Jesus Christ. He overcame death, hell and the grave once and for all. He used VICTORY to defeat the enemy and cause us to live the abundant life. However, we too must choose LIFE and not look back to the old life as we grow in the grace and knowledge of the love of God. It was His *loving kindness* which caused Him to love us so much that he made a way for freedom in the midst of an ugly world.

Galatians 5:1 exhorts us to stand fast in the freedom Christ has given us and not to submit to a yoke of slavery again. Lot's wife chose death, but we choose LIFE! We choose freedom! We choose to receive the *kindness* of the Lord and walk in His goodness.

Prayer for the Day

Father, thank you for Your loving kindness! It truly is better than anything we can imagine. Thank you for Your cleansing love that empowers us to live in victory each day! Amen!

Loving Kindness

*"Because thy loving kindness is better
than life, my lips shall praise thee."*
Psalms 63:3 (RSV)

As we grow in the grace and knowledge of the Lord Jesus Christ and see the reflection of Father God in His life, we begin to comprehend how deep, how wide, how strong, how powerful is the loving kindness of God for each of us.

In the 1970's we sang:

> *Thy loving kindness is better than life!*
> *Thy loving kindness is better than life!*
> *My lips shall praise thee; thus will I bless thee.*
> *I will lift up my hands in thy name!*

Through the years this chorus has carried me through many hard places. In January 1995, John was admitted to the hospital for open-heart surgery. Our home was located about an hour from where he was, so a friend offered their home to me just a few blocks from the hospital. I had to drive home to get my clothes, take care of some details with my mom who was living with us at the time, make arrangements for a substitute teacher, etc. The next morning while returning to the hospital, the above chorus repeated itself in my mind. Breaking into singing, I sang as loudly as I could my confession of God's unending love for John and for me. In the car that morning, God and I joined our hearts in unity to stand fast during the challenge around us. His loving-kindness truly was better than life!

When I arrived at the hospital, John and I shared together this same chorus and the joy the Lord was giving us to walk in victory no matter the outcome. While John showered, we sang "Because He Lives" over and over. We truly could face tomorrow because His loving-kindness was present with us for that day - and of course, for the days that came later. We'll never forget the sweet reminder of God to our hearts to be encouraged in the day's challenges. He was more than enough!

Prayer for the Day

Thank you, Father God, for surrounding us in the dark places of our lives with Your immeasurable loving-kindness! Our hearts are filled with praise for Your very life inside of us! Amen!

Safety of God's Kindness

*"Blessed be the LORD: for he hath shewed me
his marvelous kindness in a strong city."*
Psalms 31:21 (KJV)

How many of us have felt besieged lately with all that is going on in our world? Some have said to us their finances are failing; others say their children are wayward; and others are uncertain of safety in their own homes.

In Psalm 31 David is crying out to the Lord. His trust is totally in the Lord God Almighty; yet he experiences doubt, fear and worry. As the fear or worry tries to overwhelm him, he constantly declares the goodness of the Lord. He declares God is his shelter, his deliverer, his Lord and says He has placed David in a broad place. Finally, he says:

"*Love the Lord all you his saints!
The Lord preserves the faithful . . .
Be strong, and let your heart take courage,*
all you who wait for the Lord!" Ps. 31:24 (RSV)

Today, we declare God is our source, who loves us more than words can express. God is our strength and our song in the midst of a difficult place. God is more than able to give us the courage to stand fast in HIM.

Prayer for the Day

Thank you, Father, for being my own strength! Thank you for encouraging me no matter what is going on in my life. I choose to keep my faith and trust in You! Amen!

Kindness on our Tongue

*"She opens her mouth with skillful and godly Wisdom, and in her tongue is the law of **kindness** - giving counsel and instruction.""*

Proverbs 31:26 (RSV)

As we have pondered the kindness of the Lord in our lives and the fruit of kindness in our daily walk, let's think for a moment about **speaking with kindness** - the fruit of lips giving thanks.

Proverbs 31 is a beautiful analogy of the Church in her full beauty. We normally think of the Proverbs 31 woman, but if we add all the Church (Petra) to the description given in these verses, we are all challenged to walk this Christian walk with gracious goodness.

How many of us in correcting someone have lost our patience and used harsh words rather than speaking with kindness? How many of us have spoken harshly to a phone representative who calls unsolicited - especially during suppertime? Well, our mouth may be the evidence of our Christian walk. Ouch! When I speak harshly, I hurt another human being - by bruising a child with words, causing anger in a teenager, upsetting a store clerk or possibly frustrating my own spouse.

When Jesus Christ corrected His disciples, He spoke with kindness, patience, and love. Even though He asked, (Loosely interpreted),"How long must I put up with you guys?" He continued to teach them and lead them by his own example. I believe kindness for those He was teaching poured from His lips - words of acceptance, healing, strength, joy, love, and kindness. Let's take on the demeanor of Jesus Christ through our spoken words.

Prayer for the Day

Father, help us to reflect Your kindness everywhere we are - in our homes, in our churches, in our communities. May our mouths be filled with continual praise so that the words that proceed from us will be full of kindness, reaping love and joy for others! Amen!

Soft Answer

"A soft answer turns away wrath; but grievous words stir up anger."

Proverbs 15:1 (RSV)

In rearing children, we often hear "Watch your tone!" when a child talks back or uses one of those inflections in the voice that causes one to put up a guard. In the movie *Mary Poppins*, she sang "A Spoonful of Sugar" to play with the children and to persuade them to do things her way. She was a pro at making the sour moments sweet.

Honestly, when our daughters were teenagers, our lives would have been much simpler if I'd reacted kindly instead of demandingly in conversations with them. I remember one occasion as Ginger and I were in a heated discussion when I realized I had lost my temper and was screaming at her. (I'm not sure why we think others can understand us better if we yell.) Suddenly, the Holy Spirit spoke quietly to me, "Back off. Treat her with love, not anger." The moment I did, she too quieted down. Of course, I had to apologize to her and ask her forgiveness. No matter how she acted, I was the adult in the situation and should have been setting her an example of love, kindness, and patience.

Truly kindness, soft answers, and gentleness win more people than anger, impatience, or heated discussions ever did. Another plus to using the soft answer is that one never has to apologize for a kind response. In that way we save time, we invest in someone's life, and we are joyful as we complete a conversation or a confrontation.

Prayer for the Day

Thank you, Father, for giving us the power to speak in a soft tone and to use kindness everywhere we are, especially in our own homes. Amen!

Goodness

"But the fruit of the Spirit is love, joy, peace, patience, kindness, goodness. . ."

Galatians 5:22

God Is Good

*"But the fruit of the Spirit is love, joy, peace, patience, kindness, **goodness**…"*

Galatians 5:22 (RSV)

As we have been studying the fruit of the Holy Spirit over these past weeks, my daily acts have taken on new power. When I speak out of turn, I am immediately convicted. When I lose my patience, I am immediately reminded of God's power to do the work in me. If my peace is threatened, I dig my faith into WHOSE I am and stand my ground with more strength than ever before.

As we consider ***goodness***, the following song comes to my heart:

God is good . . . all the time
He put a song of praise in this heart of mine
God is good, God is good
All the time!

Whenever we're in a Christian gathering, one can say "God is good!" and the response will be "All the time!" We as believers began to let that truth sink deeply into our lives. However, when tragedies occur or the money gets tight, the doubts arise. What if? Maybe not? Am I really sure?

The goodness of God is never up for discussion. HE IS GOOD!!!!!!! He loves us!!!!! He had a plan from the foundation of the world to bless us with **HIS GOODNESS** as well as His loving kindness. Over and over the Word of God reminds us of His goodness. When Peter spoke before the Sanhedrin in Acts 4, he told the religious leaders of the day that he spoke with the Name of Jesus, the power of Jesus, and the authority of Jesus! He always saw Jesus **doing good,** so that's what he and John had done on the temple steps - giving good to the crippled man, who was walking and leaping and praising God because of Father's goodness to heal.

Prayer for the Day

*Thank you, Father, You are GOOD! Thank you for Your **goodness** toward us even when we didn't know we needed it! Thank you for granting us **goodness** all the days of our lives. May we be examples of that **goodness** on the face of the earth today! Amen!*

All Goodness

"For ye were once darkness, but now ye are light in the Lord: walk as children of light (for the fruit of the Spirit is in all goodness, righteousness, and truth;) proving what is acceptable to the Lord.""
Ephesians 5:8-10 (KJV)

We must truly walk as children of the light. Many in today's world would tell us that goodness and light come from within us, but we KNOW that GOODNESS proceeded from God Almighty from the foundation of the earth. His plan was for great fellowship and companionship with His children. In the Garden of Eden, He walked with His creation and talked with them as His own. Even though He was rejected, He came again in the form of Jesus Christ to restore us to FULL and COMPLETE companionship with Him.

Nothing can separate us from the love of God in Christ Jesus. (Romans 8) However, we often separate ourselves by buying into the world's view of our magnanimous God. Remember, nothing is too hard for Him. Nothing is more important than seeking Him. Nothing can replace Him. Nothing can dethrone Him. Nothing can overcome Him. He OVERCAME all the evil and brought us only GOODNESS, mercy and love.

Prayer for the Day

Father, we thank you for Your GOODNESS! Thank you it is ours every day! You are AWESOME, INCREDIBLE, WORTHY, and GOOD! We love you! Amen!

Surely Goodness

*"Surely goodness and mercy shall follow
me all the days of my life;
And I shall dwell in the house of the Lord forever."*
Psalms 23:6 (RSV)

All of us are very familiar with this marvelous scripture, but I wonder how many times we think of what the very goodness of God is. Do we consider as the young boys who were walking home from school with two people following him: One said, "I don't know who's following us." The other replied, "I sure do! It's Surely, Goodness and Mercy. They follow me all the days of my life."

He had been told over and over and over again about this verse of scripture. He maybe didn't understand the full implications of his answer, but we can comprehend what it means. No matter what comes our way, God's goodness and mercy follow us!

Joyce Meyer said on her program: "God's gone before you! And he's got your back!" Yes, He has paved the way for us to go forward where He has placed us. He has made a way where there doesn't seem to be a way. Psalm 91 promises us protection at every turn - every step we take we take in HIM!

Whatever is going on in life today, just remember goodness and mercy are following you, keeping you safe, surrounding you with love, and covering every step you take in Him!

Prayer for the Day

Thank you, Lord God, for being my forward mantle and my rear guard! Amen!

Abundant Goodness

*"O how abundant is thy goodness, which thou
hast laid up for those who fear thee,
And wrought for those who take refuge in
thee, in the sight of the sons of men!"*
Psalms 31:19 (RSV)

As we meditate upon the goodness of the Lord, we can remember the times where He has blessed us abundantly when we were least expecting it. When I held our first baby in my arms, I was totally overwhelmed with the love that flowed through me. Suddenly I began to understand how much my parents had loved me and how deeply God loved me. That moment began a journey of sold-out love for my family that changed my life. Even though I'd had some idea that I was loved, I was not aware of the ABUNDANCE of that love. Bathe in that love - that pure goodness of God Almighty's grace poured out for each of us. Crawl up in His lap like a small child to allow Him to hold you close and comfort you.

Behold what manner of love the Father has given unto us in I John 3:1 that we should be called the children of God. When He thought of us, His heart was overwhelmed with love for each of us. He loves us enough to care for us, lead us, correct us, and sustain us in whatever life throws our way just like we want to protect, help and love our own children. We can trust His goodness!

Dr. Ralph Martin from King's Vineyard Church in Stockbridge, GA, pointed out the only difference between the words *God* and *good* is that *good* has one more "o." Notice that "good" is an extension of God's name, actually a double portion of who He is in us!

Prayer for the Day

Lord God, help us to receive Your pure goodness and trust You completely in all we do! Amen!

Lean on His Goodness

"For indeed we have had the glad tidings [of God] proclaimed to us just as truly as they [the Israelites of old did when the good news of deliverance from bondage came to them]; but the message they heard did not benefit them, because it was not mixed with faith [that is, with the leaning of the entire personality on God in absolute trust and confidence in His power, wisdom and goodness] by those who heard it; neither were they united in faith with [Joshua and Caleb] the ones who heard [did believe]."
Hebrews 4:2 (AMP)

Wow! If we just chew on that verse the remainder of the day, we'll have enough fuel to live in great victory, never doubting God's love for us. However, most of us read and then forget, so let's think for a minute about the definition of *faith* in the Amplified Bible.

Faith is *with the leaning of the entire personality on God in absolute trust and confidence in His power, wisdom and* ***goodness.*** That's the God kind of faith for sure. First, we must *believe him*, then we can *trust him*, but can you picture yourself really *leaning* on HIM?

Think about a big oak tree when you could lean your back into the tree and know it was going to hold you up no matter what wind blew. Our faith is that capable if we truly believe GOD IS GOOD! Say out loud, "My God is good! My God loves me! My God cares for me! My God is capable of doing good all my life! My God has provided goodness for me every day! My God is GOOD! His mercies are new every morning!

Prayer for the Day

Thank you, Jesus, for making a way for the goodness of Father to be experienced upon the earth in us! Amen!

Absolute Trust and Confidence

"For indeed we have had the glad tidings [of God] proclaimed to us just as truly as they [the Israelites of old did when the good news of deliverance from bondage came to them]; but the message they heard did not benefit them, because it was not mixed with faith [that is, with the leaning of the entire personality on God in absolute trust and confidence in His power, wisdom and goodness] by those who heard it; neither were they united in faith with [Joshua and Caleb] the ones who heard [did believe]."
Hebrews 4:2 (AMP)

In meditating on Hebrews 4:2, one cannot ignore the "absolute trust and confidence" required of faith. Peter teaches in his second epistle that faith is the beginning of all growth. Without faith, we cannot even come into the Kingdom of God because we must have at least a little bit in order to accept Jesus as our Lord. It is in the acceptance that our love begins to grow for Him.

Now, as we grow we have to learn to trust Him completely just like I can trust the ground to hold me up. When I climb a ladder, it seems very shaky to me. I always have to make certain it will not tip me over and dump me out. Standing in faith is much the same way. We have to know that we know we can TRUST the Lord God Almighty. After all, He created the universe, knows how everything works together, is a firm foundation, and fully trustworthy.

So I have to say to my mind, "I will trust in the name of the Lord my God. Nothing can shake me from my established faith in him. His reputation goes before Him. I can lean on Him in ABSOLUTE TRUST AND CONFIDENCE in His goodness, fully persuaded of His love and power in my life." As I confess His goodness, the doubts flee and His never ending love transcends the unrest and brings peace.

Prayer for the Day

Thank you, Father, for Your always being the same - yesterday, today, and forever! Amen!

Faithfulness

"But the fruit of the Spirit is love, joy, peace, patience, kindness, goodness, faithfulness..."
Galatians 5:22

Faithfulness

*"But the fruit of the Spirit is love, joy, peace, patience, kindness, goodness, **faithfulness** . . ."*
Galatians 5:22 (RSV)

The fruit of **faithfulness** becomes a part of our lives as we imitate the Word of God spoken on the face of the earth. God's Word is true. He always does what he says; He watches over His people always; He never gives up on us even when we may not do everything right; He sent His only Son so that we could live in victory; and His promises are always yes and amen! (2 Cor. 1:20)

The Lord taught me many lessons through the years, but one of the most practical was telling the truth! Just after I was filled with the Holy Spirit, I began to see how much I exaggerated everything. The minute I would say, "There were 40 people there," I would feel a nudge - "I believe there were only 30." Or I might say, "I'd love to come!" but in my mind I was dreading the event. The Holy Spirit began to work on my truth-telling. He convicted me when I was really lying, showing me a more excellent way - His way of **faithfulness.** There were other times when I knew I wasn't telling the truth, but I'd say it anyway. Oh, my, talk about a person under construction.

Now forty years later, speaking the truth is a way of life for me. I finally have the courage to be myself, not to pretend to be someone else or do something because someone else expects me to say it their way. I have hidden His Word in my heart that I might not sin against Him. He is a God of truth. After all, Jesus said, "I am the way, the truth, and the life . . ." Thank God for loving me so much that He is changing me from the inside out. . . His **faithfulness** to us is amazing!

Prayer for the Day

*Lord, I come to You. Forgive me when I just try to get by. Show me any weakness in my life and help the words that come out of my mouth carry only **truthfulness** at every turn. Amen!*

Faithful God

*"But the Lord is faithful; he will strengthen
you and guard you from evil."*
2 Thessalonians 3:3 (RSV)

We learn faithfulness from observing the faithfulness of our Father God. When He speaks a Word, He fulfills it. When He created the universe, He did so with His spoken Word. *"He said, Let there be light."* (Gen. 1:3) When He promises us something, we can trust Him.

Jesus told his disciples he would go away but in three days he would be resurrected. They had great difficulty believing that, especially during the crucifixion. However, when Peter and John went to the empty tomb in John 20 and then saw Jesus in Galilee, they were more than totally convinced of the fact that when Jesus told them something, it would indeed come to pass.

We need to grasp the fact that God loves us so much, He will keep us from evil in these days if we listen to His voice, obey what He tells us to do, and rest in His promises. If we read it in His Word, He will perform it - maybe not in our time or in our way, but HE WILL DO IT as His eternal plan unfolds for His people.

Prayer for the Day

Father, grant us faithfulness to keep on believing no matter what we see around us, to keep on standing when things seem rough, and to keep on spreading light in the world even though darkness is all around us! Amen!

Our Faithfulness

*". . . I have loved you with an everlasting love;
therefore I have continued my faithfulness to you."*
Jeremiah 31:3 (RSV)

We cannot doubt the faithfulness of God. He has shown himself faithful to every promise in his Word. However, we often find ourselves wavering in our decisions. The world calls us to follow after the news as it's given, the new agendas of other people, the expectations of our families, and the demands of those in authority over us. But we are called to heed the voice of the Lord God and listen to no other.

When I become tempted to listen to what the world is saying, I have to draw back to the Word of God. Choosing to read his Word, spend time in his presence, and seek his direction for my life brings me peace in the midst of hectic circumstances. Following hard after God is a choice of one's will.

Choosing to remain faithful to the Lord God Almighty is a decision we make every day. Am I going to do what so and so wants or am I going to keep myself in the middle of the will of Father for me? The only way I can stay steady is to remain in his presence each day, walk with him by my side always, and CHOOSE TO FOLLOW his example of being faithful in all things.

Prayer for the Day

Father, thank you for centering my vision upon You! Thank you for Your unending faithfulness. I want faithfulness to be a fruit of my own daily life. Amen!

What Is Faithfulness?

"Now faith is the assurance of things hoped for, the conviction of things not seen."
Hebrews 11:1 (RSV)

When we consider the faith that is covered in Hebrews 11:1, we often consider something we have to reach for - the God kind of faith if you will. However, let's ponder today about how our faith grows.

After receiving salvation, one should begin to study the Gospel of John in order to realize the depth, height and breadth of the love of God for each of us. It is in the studying and meditating on His unending love that we begin to grasp His faithfulness toward us. Then we gain an impetus which begins to thrust us forward in trusting Him with all we are, all we have and all we do.

Faithfulness signifies that I am willing to persevere through the daily grind to bring glory and honor to my Father God! Faithfulness is the outpouring of my love for Him as I serve in my home, my community and my church. Faithfulness is the attribute given to us by the Holy Spirit to stand strong in our convictions to do what is right and Godly at every turn in the road. Faithfulness grants us the power to never give up, to never give in, to hold on tightly to the love of God in all circumstances and to rejoice in our hope of His presence. Faithfulness is the fruit of a life well-lived!

Prayer for the Day

Thank you, Father, that You even made provision for my faithfulness. All I have to do is appropriate Your faithfulness in me to walk on in power each day! Amen!

Because Christ Lives

"Repent, for the kingdom of heaven is at hand."
Matthew 3:2 (RSV)

God's faithfulness is evident in John the Baptist as he preached the kingdom of heaven is at hand. He quoted from Isaiah, the Messianic prophet declaring "one will come." At that moment, John declared, "He has come!"

This blessed appearance of Christ on the earth assures us God does exactly what He says He will do. He spoke the world into being . . . He gave His only begotten Son so that we could be a part of the kingdom of heaven. He did exactly what He said He would do. When Jesus stepped on the scene in baptism in Matthew 3, He was fulfilling God's Word. Isaiah told us one will come as a shoot of Jesse to free us from all sin and degradation. Jesus is the ONE. He came! He lived! He conquered death and the grave! Hallelujah! Jesus is alive!

"Because He lives, I can face tomorrow" rings out in Bill and Gloria Gaither's music. "Because He lives, all fear is gone. Because I know, I know who holds the future, and life is worth the living just because Christ lives."

Prayer for the Day

Father, thank you we can trust Your faithfulness because You always do exactly what You promise. We can count on You at every turn in the road. We can be Your people, called by Your name because of Your faithful promises to us! Amen!

Faithfulness of Jesus

"Then Jesus, knowing all that was about to befall Him, went out to them and said, Whom are you seeking - Whom do you want? They (soldiers and guards) answered Him, Jesus the Nazarene. Jesus said to them, I AM HE..."
John 18:5-6 (AMP)

We celebrate the life given for us through faithfulness to His call every Easter. Jesus willingly lay down His life so that we might have life abundantly! Once He settled His battle with Father in the Garden of Gethsemane, He never looked back. When the soldiers came with Judas to arrest Him, He did not flinch. He did not hide. He did not fight. He said "I AM HE."

Knowing exactly what was about to befall Him, He willingly walked the walk silently to the house of Caiaphas; then, He spent the night in prison, stood trial, suffered the beatings and mocking before He willingly finished the journey to the cross. The faithfulness of Jesus shows us how to live out our lives. No matter what comes our way, we have the power within us to walk as Jesus walked, to live as Jesus lived, to lay down our lives when necessary for the good of others. We can be faithful because His faithfulness is His gift to us.

Prayer for the Day

Father, thank you for Your faithfulness in sending Your Son. Lord Jesus, thank you for Your faithfulness in walking out Your destiny. Holy Spirit, thank you for the power You bring to help us live a life of faithfulness each day! Amen!

Father's Faithfulness

*"I will say of the Lord He is my refuge
and my fortress, my God,
on Him I lean and rely, and in Him I (confidently) trust!"*
Psalms 91:2 (AMP)

This morning as I meditated on God's protection for us by shielding us, covering us, providing for us and for being with us each moment of every day through the resurrection power of the Lord Jesus Christ, I have been overwhelmed by Father's faithfulness!

Throughout my Harper Study Bible, I have underlined scriptures with the names of those I love in the margin. In 1974 for our move to Tennessee, in 1988 for our daughter's life and freedom, in 1990 for the provision of Godly men for our daughters to marry, in 2000 for the life of our granddaughter, for John's jobs in 1974, 1984, and 1989 when he was laid off. WOW! GOD IS FAITHFUL!

All His promises for those who walk after His name in obedience and submission unto Him will be covered over by HIS FULL PROVISION! Let's remain in His care.

Prayer for the Day

Thank you, Father, for Your faithfulness to all generations. May ours be one to leave a legacy of love, an example of strength and a life well-lived in Your presence! Amen!

Develop Faithfulness

"Lean on, trust and be confident in the Lord with all your heart and mind, and do not rely on your own insight or understanding."
Proverbs 3:5 (AMP)

We know God is faithful, but how to we develop the fruit of faithfulness in our own lives? First we have to commit our ways to the Lord God. We are exhorted to lean on Him in all our ways. For me this has had to come through practice and knowing He'll do what He says.

There's an old saying, "God said it and I believe it. That settles it." Well, it's really more than my believing it. God said it and that settles it. My doubt comes because my "believer" is not exercised enough to grasp the full power of His Word and His love for me. Therefore, I've been practicing for over fifty years!

As a child, we are taught "practice makes perfect," and even though I cannot totally agree that perfection comes here on earth, my walk has become easier because I no longer struggle with WHO IS IN CHARGE. God is! That settles it! Practice! Practice! Practice! Just like any exercise program, the muscles of faith are made stronger each day! We will be ready when we meet Him in the air! (Philippians 1:6)

Prayer for the Day

Father, when doubts and fears assail my thinking, help me remember You are more than enough. You created the universe. Certainly, You can care for me and mine! Thank you! Amen!

He's in Charge

"In all your ways know, recognize and acknowledge Him, and He will direct and make straight and plain your paths."
Proverbs 3:6 (AMP)

When we consider the faithfulness of God, many of us quote the above verse without giving it much thought. Read it again, emphasizing all the pronouns referring to Jehovah God. He will direct; He will make straight; He will make plain. None of those are suggestions. They are all declarative, positive statements.

Often I am tempted to take over and "make things happen" myself. This verse reminds me "HE WILL DO IT!" I must be obedient to what He tells me to do. I must be faithful over that which He has given me to care for. I must offer my life to Him to work through me. BUT HE IS THE ONE WHO COMPLETES THE TASK!

As we ponder His power, let's offer ourselves anew to Him to be used mightily in His kingdom to fulfill His purpose on the earth for our lives. Let's fall back into His everlasting arms and rest in His inherent goodness, faithfulness, and love.

Prayer for the Day

Wow, God, You are great and greatly to be praised! Thank you for always finishing what You call me to do. Thank you for Your faithfulness working inside of me to fulfill Your call on my life. Praise to Your holy, righteous NAME! You truly are more than enough! Amen.

Preserved

*"Love the Lord, all you his saints!
The Lord preserves the faithful,*

. . . .

*Be strong, and let your heart take courage,
all you who wait for the Lord!"*

Psalms 31:23-24 (RSV)

How glorious is the truth "the Lord preserves the faithful"? Webster's define *preserve* as "to keep safe: guard, protect; to keep from decaying; maintain." Interesting idea this preservation process! God kept his chosen people safe throughout the Old Testament until He sent His only Son to make a permanent *preservation* for us all!

Every summer I made strawberry preserves. How my family loved them on homemade bread! They were especially delicious at Christmas - some eight months after their preparation. We'd open the jar, smell the sweetness and spread it on our biscuits! Yum!

One time, I opened a jar that hadn't been sufficiently sealed with paraffin. There was a slight leak in the covering and yuck! What a terrible odor emanated from that jar! I was always very careful to keep the preserves covered because I knew they'd spoil if I didn't, but that one day, I had left the berries open to the outside influence of the air around them. Oops!

We must make certain we are dwelling in the shelter of the Most High God because it is in that safe hiding place we are preserved by Him in our faithfulness. Our first priority must be to remain fixed under His glorious covering!

Prayer for the Day

Thank you, Father God, for being my shelter, my high tower, my covering, and my preserver of life in every day! May the people who catch my scent smell Your sweet aroma of love! Amen!

Faithful Servant

"Let your loins be girded and your lamps burning..."
Luke 12:35 (RSV)

Just following this exhortation of Jesus on waiting for His second coming, He teaches a powerful parable on the faithful servant. He comments in Luke 12:43 *"Blessed is that servant whom his master when he comes will find him so doing."* That is serving others with the very best one has to share, whether that be food, clothing, shelter, time, effort, or commitment. The faithful servant gives all he has to show love on the face of the earth through reaching out to touch someone else with a caring hand.

When we commit to follow hard after God, it takes the fruit of faithfulness to continue when the road becomes difficult to travel. Each one of us has to make the choice to press forward. Faithfulness keeps our eyes on Jesus Christ and His calling, not on the circumstances around us. Faithfulness keeps us focused on the voice of the Lord and listening to no other. Faithfulness keeps us encouraged to stand our ground to see the goodness of God in the land of the living!

Prayer for the Day

Thank you, Father, for Your faithfulness to us! Thank you we can wait expectantly because we know You're with us each day! Thank you for the extra strength to fulfill Your daily call on our livesl. Amen!

Continue in Faithfulness

*"He who is faithful in a very little
is faithful also in much…"*

Luke 16:10 (RSV)

Faithfulness sometimes is grown slowly. When we come into the Kingdom of God, we begin serving wherever we are. I started teaching the Word to nursery children when I was about eight years old. By the time I was twelve I was helping in junior high with our Pastor's wife. When I was 17, I was helping plan college-age studies. Little by little God gives us opportunities to be faithful.

One thing I've learned is that when I sign up to help or to work, I need to show up on time with a "happy heart." So many times we commit to do something, but other things rise to take our focus off our commitments. God is not honored when we lose our integrity by not following through with commitments. He has really expected me to show up places I thought were going to be too difficult to fulfill, but once I give my word to do something, I must honor that word at all costs to myself unless there is an emergency situation. When I arrive at the "commitment spot," the power and strength and anointing to fulfill that call comes so mightily that God is honored in the day!

Through the years, I've observed that when we are faithful in the nitty-gritty, daily commitments, God calls us to serve in more challenging places. In the beginning, the new spots may not be comfortable, but training takes time. Time brings wisdom. Wisdom brings confidence. Confidence leads us on to the next step. As we grow in maturity, He trusts us with more and more in His Kingdom. As well, we trust Him in us!

Prayer for the Day

Thank you, Father, for teaching me to be faithful every day in my family so that I could be Your faithful servant, truly willing to lay down my life as a living sacrifice unto You! Amen!

Remain Faithful

"When he (Barnabas) came and saw the grace of God, he was glad; and he exhorted them all to remain faithful to the Lord with steadfast purpose; for he was a good man, full of the Holy Spirit and of faith."
Acts 11:23-24a (RSV)

When the leaders in Acts went forth to new converts, they reminded them to remain *faithful* and *steadfast.* How amazing that today we are urged in the same way to continue to do that which God has called us to do. Remain steadfast in your calling - that which the Lord has placed in your hands to accomplish.

How do we remain steadfast when the times continue to be difficult around us, throwing our thoughts to the needs of the day rather than the provision of God? We have to choose just like the early converts to do whatever it takes to hold fast to our confession of faith, which is Jesus Christ is the same yesterday, today, and forever. Jesus Christ resurrected from the grave and gave us the power to live in victory. We choose VICTORY over defeat. We choose JOY over mourning. We choose PEACE over strife. We choose PATIENCE over agitation. We choose KINDNESS over rudeness. We choose GOODNESS over meanness. We choose FAITHFULNESS over giving up. We STAND!

Prayer for the Day

Thank you, Father, for making a way for us to remain stable and fixed, inaccessible in the secret place of the Most High! Amen!

Wait on the Lord

"I believe that I shall see the goodness of the Lord in the land of the living! Wait for the Lord; be strong, and let your heart take courage; yea, wait for the Lord."
Psalms 27:13-14 (RSV)

Faithfulness requires that we stand our ground, keep our eyes on the Lord Jesus, and never be moved by what we see - only what He shows us to do. Often, that is difficult to maintain over the long haul. However, it is when we set our face like flint and are faithful in the daily routine of life that we see His power bring breakthrough over and over and over again!

When we moved to East Tennessee in 1974, it took a while for our home in Titusville to sell. We lived with my parents for a year while building our new home. No one wanted to lend us money because we didn't have permanent jobs. No one wanted to hire us because we had been gone for many years. As we stood on this marvelous promise from Ps. 27, we saw God intervene in our lives.

First, He reminded us that it took a miracle to put the stars in place and He was the one who had done it! As the months passed, He helped us put the new house on the hill, He brought in jobs for John and for me, He cared for every detail of the journey, and just when we thought the house in Titusville would never sell, IT DID! God is FAITHFUL! He wants us to remain fixed upon His face - seeking the Giver and not the gift, searching for His peace in the midst of every temptation to wander or give up!

Prayer for the Day

Thank you, Lord God, You are MORE THAN ENOUGH! Help me keep my focus on You and Your great promises! Amen!

Gentleness

"But the fruit of the Spirit is love, joy, peace, patience, kindness, goodness, faithfulness, gentleness . . ."

Galatians 5:22

Gentleness

> *"But the fruit of the Spirit is love, joy, peace, patience, kindness, goodness, faithfulness, **gentleness** . . ."*
> **Galatians 5:23-24a (RSV)**

Gentleness, Gentleness if what I long for.
Gentleness is what I need.
Gentleness is what you want from me.
Take my life and form it.
Take my mind, transform it.
Take my will, conform it . . .
To Yours, to Yours, Oh, Lord!

Gentleness seems to be a by-product of *faithfulness*. Of course, some of us are gentle by nature, but that wasn't true for me. I was more like a bull in a china shop because I can look at a situation, see what needs to happen, and want to go right ahead with the plan. Therefore, I would press on to complete the task set before me at full speed. Usually I didn't stop to consider that others might want to move in another way, but as I began to grow in the fruit of the Spirit, the Lord began to show me not to be in such a hurry to rush in where angels fear to tread. He began to show me how to listen to the hearts of others and respond with a softness that was new to me.

We've all heard the expression, "Speak softly but carry a big stick." Honestly, I think I carried the big stick and spoke with too much authority in my younger life. Of course, I still take authority in situations because that is a gift in my life, but I am learning to be gentler along the way and to be gentler in my approach. Webster defines *gentle* as 1) of, relating to, or characteristic of a gentleman; 2) kind, amiable 3) tractable, docile 4) not harsh, stern or violent, 5) soft, delicate, 6) moderate.

Prayer for the Day

Lord, please grow within us Your gentleness. Help us to revere others more than ourselves. Help us to take on Your quiet, gentle Spirit so that others may be drawn to us for love and mercy! Amen.

Be Gentle!

"Remind them to be submissive to rulers and authorities, to be obedient, to be ready for any honest work, to speak evil of no one, to avoid quarreling, to be gentle, and to show perfect courtesy toward all men."
Titus 3:1-2 (RSV)

Ummmm! This is an amazing scripture when you think about the gentleness of one's spirit. Many of us don't want to submit to others much less be gentle with the ones with whom we do not agree.

Growing up my siblings and I argued about many things. If one said something was black, the other one might declare it to be white - just to be right. As we matured into adulthood, we still had heated discussions. However, the Lord began to train me to have a quieter spirit. I'll have to admit this took a long time, but I am getting better and better all the time and strive always to take the other person into account before reacting.

Charles Stanley taught one Sunday recently on how to deal with confrontations. He said he had learned to keep a quiet spirit when others attacked him, realizing their outbreak of anger was not about him or even really aimed at him. Many times others are dealing with such hurt in their own lives that all they know to do is lash out at whoever is handy.

As believers, we are to develop a gentle, quiet spirit, knowing God is working in our hearts to change each one of us into his own image. Just think, when they spat in the face of our Savior, He said not a word!

Prayer for the Day

Oh, Father, we can hardly imagine the pure gentleness of Your spirit. Help us to grow in Your strength, character, and integrity that we too might deal with others in gentleness. Amen!

A Gentle and Quiet Spirit

"But let it be the hidden person of the heart with the imperishable jewel of a gentle and quiet spirit, which in God's sight is very precious."
I Peter 3:4 (AMP)

What an amazing thought in today's world! Peter was teaching the women of his day not to be consumed with the adorning of the hair, the decorations of gold, and the wearing of clothing. I can't imagine what Peter would say in our world today. However, I believe he would say the same thing as he did then - to wear the precious jewel of a gentle, quiet spirit.

When our children were in their teen years, somehow I thought they could hear me better if I would just speak louder - maybe sometimes even shout. ☺ However, they only wanted to shout back. But when we learn to be still and know that He is God, we can speak softly, wait patiently, and gently love the one who is upset around us. We are to set the tone for the presence of God!

One day this week I was in a position where one of the people was just overwrought. She was saying things I couldn't believe, accusing people with lies, and really making a ridiculous situation for everyone. All I could do was be quiet, pray and wait on the Holy Spirit to give me the strength to be WISE. I kept my mouth shut and others around did as well. The upset person quieted. No one responded. The irrational behavior ceased! Glory to God!

Prayer for the Day

Lord God, thank you for still working on me to make me what You want me to be. You created the moon and stars and You're still working on me. Thank you for not letting up until I become Your vessel of honor on the earth! Amen!

With Gentleness of Christ

"I, Paul, myself entreat you, by the meekness and gentleness of Christ - I who am humble when face to face with you, but bold to you when I am away!"
II Corinthians 10:1 (RSV)

Even Paul who was often so bold that he knocked the socks off the ones listening exhorts us to have the meekness and gentleness of Christ. I am reminded of when the Pharisees wanted to stone the woman for adultery. Jesus sat calmly, waiting for the right words when he said, "Let the one without sin cast the first stone." Amazing!

So many times I run ahead, do not wait upon the Lord for the right words, and plunge into what I perceive to be the best action. However, Jesus was strong, firm, and gentle all at the same time. He knew His Father. He knew that the situation didn't threaten Him. He knew He who had no sin could recognize and give forgiveness. How gentle - to offer forgiveness where there was none, to offer kindness when others wanted to kill, to offer love in the midst of rejection.

Just as Jesus offers those precious gifts to us, let's offer them to others.

Prayer for the Day

Oh, Father, grant that we may take on the gentleness of Your precious Son. Help us to be humbled in Your presence, changed by Your grace, and filled with Your love. Amen!

Spirit of Gentleness

"Brethren, if a man is overtaken in any trespass, you who are spiritual should restore him in a spirit of gentleness. Look to yourself, lest you too be tempted."
Galatians 6:1 (RSV)

Many times believers quote the above verse with the idea that it is our job to correct all those who are doing wrong or making mistakes with their lives. Notice how that correction is to be done "with a spirit of gentleness."

Ummmm! That throws a new slant on correction not only in the Body of Christ but also in our own families as well as extended families. So many times we take the "holier than thou" attitude when what we should do is "bear one another's burdens" (Gal. 6:2) with God's great love.

That doesn't mean that we embrace the wrong someone is doing. It means we embrace the hurting person. One never knows the bruises, pain, and suffering in someone's heart that drives them to make wrong choices. When someone is living in sin or practicing wrong doing, go to the Lord in prayer about that person. Ask Him to give you a heart of love for him/her and expect Him to give you love and not judgment as you deal with others.

Just like Jesus said, "Let the one without sin cast the first stone." If we truly love one another as God loves us, then we'll have the gentleness to deal in love and not in the flesh.

Prayer for the Day

Oh, Father, grant that I may seek to love and forgive. May I offer help and not hurt everywhere I am. I appropriate Your gentleness within me for this very day! Amen!

The Gentle Nurse

But we were gentle among you, like a nurse taking care of her children."

I Thess. 2:7 (RSV)

Thinking of the Apostle Paul as a gentle person takes imagination because we see him as a definite, strong, determined leader in the early church. However, he says in this verse that he was gentle with the new believers in training them to grow in the grace and knowledge of the Lord Jesus Christ.

When our second daughter was born, her tiny body was covered with eczema from neck to toes. To lay her on hospital sheets took her skin off, so we left the hospital less than 24 hours after her birth to get her into softer, gentler clothes and blankets. For the first six weeks of her life, we bathed her with baby oil and aloe because her skin couldn't tolerate soap and water. We wrapped her in 100% cotton blankets, laid her on soft towels or sheets, changed her cotton diapers often to keep her flesh protected, and waited for her skin to heal.

As the years passed, she continued to require special soaps, shampoo, clothing, etc. She could never go barefoot because her skin would crack open, so she wore cotton socks all the time. We found treatment for her through the Word of God, dermatologists, as well as faith in God's healing power through time.

Never once did we resent caring for her in such special ways. Father God is the same. He is gentle with us and we should be gentle with others. The gentle touch can heal a wounded heart or help heal a broken body. Gentleness is one of the sweetest gifts of the Holy Spirit. If we cared for one another like we would our own baby girl, what a marvelous world this would be!

Prayer for the Day

Father, create within us a gentle, quiet spirit that allows Your love to flow to others to carry healing in our hands as we reach out to touch others. Amen!

Come Unto Me

"Come to me, all who labor and are heavy laden, and I will give you rest. Take my yoke upon you, and learn of me; for I am gentle and lowly in heart, and you will find rest for your souls. For my yoke is easy, and my burden is light."

Mathew. 11:28-30 (RSV)

Terry MacAlmon has written a magnificent song based on this verse. Just to listen to him play the piano and sing "Come Unto Me!" makes me want to crawl into the lap of Father God and rest in His presence. That is the kind of gentleness Jesus taught the disciples to seek from God Almighty in this magnificent scripture depicting how believers can enter the presence of God with great boldness, knowing we will be accepted and loved by Him.

Jesus instructs us the only way to the Father is through the Son. He promises if we'll come to Father through the Son we will find gentleness and rest. This world offers us rejection, arguments, confusion, and stress, but Father offers us a place of refuge from the daily grind – a place where we are welcome to enter and stay as long as we choose. This kind of gentle spirit is birthed from the love of God for all mankind.

There is no reason for us to worry or fret when we can enter into the marvelous place of resting in Father's gentleness. So I've learned to make a conscious decision to lay my troubles down and go into His place of comfort, gentleness and love. That is where I find rest for my soul.

Prayer for the Day

Father, here I am to receive Your total goodness, grace, and love. Restore me with Your gentleness, heal me with Your own loving arms, and refresh Your Spirit within me so that I may find rest in this day! Amen!

Self-Control

"But the fruit of the Spirit is love, joy, peace, patience, kindness, goodness, faithfulness, gentleness, self-control . . ."

Galatians 5:22

Self-Control

"But the fruit of the Spirit is love, joy, peace, patience, kindness, goodness, faithfulness, gentleness, self-control; against such there is no law."

Galatians 5:22-23 (RSV)

Surely the goodness of the Lord God will follow us wherever we go. However, sometimes it is difficult for us to walk in that goodness 24/7. As Paul said in Romans 7:15, "*I do not understand my own actions. For I do not do what I want, but I do the very thing I hate.*" He was talking about the old man inside himself. I too have an "old woman" inside me. The more I practice, the easier it becomes, but there are still times when I don't choose to allow the Holy Spirit to flow so easily through me. Something may happen that is just the point that pushes my buttons and I allow myself to lose control.

I believe one of the reasons God sent us the Holy Spirit to teach us *self-control,* which means one's choice to 1) have the power to direct or regulate; 2) reserve, restraint; 3) a device for regulating a mechanism. When you add *self* in front of *control*, it means that power flows through us! When I look at definition three, I see that the "control" inside of me is the Holy Spirit. He is such a gentleman that I have to give Him the control button before He uses it, but when I choose to hand it over to Him, He gives me all I need! Glory to God!

Prayer for the Day

Thank you, Father, for providing ONE inside of me to teach me how to move in power and love and a sound mind! Help me learn to use Your strength to be the person You want me to be at every turn in this day! May I be strong enough to choose Your way and not my own. Amen!

Every Runner

*"Every athlete exercises self-control in
all things. They do it to receive
a perishable wreath, but we an imperishable."*
I Corinthians 5:25 (RSV)

We're all athletes of sorts in this Christian life, running the race that has been set before us in our call from God. Each one of us has to choose to practice our greatest area of need in order to become stronger each day - sometimes in each moment of the day.

Not long after I experienced the infilling of the Holy Spirit in 1970, the Lord began to convict me about the way I took care of my body as His temple. First, smoking came up. Then my doctor, who was puffing on a cigarette, said, "I think it would be a good idea for you to quit smoking." God had already been working on me . . . Then John said, "We'll just quit!" And he did!!!!!!!!!!!

That left me to work, practice, pray and cry out to God and wait - in the meantime trying to cut out the large number of cigarettes I smoked each day. This went on for seven months until finally one day when I lit up in the bathroom, I said, "God, I can't do this on my own!" He said, "I know, but I will do it for you if you'll let me." I prayed immediately, "Take this awful desire from me please!" I had cut down to that one cigarette a day, but couldn't go any further.

I threw that cigarette in the commode, got down on my knees, laying my head on the commode and cried. Finally, I was free! I threw that pack away and NEVER have I wanted another one! Praise be unto God!

I had practiced, prayed, waited, believed, cried out over and over, but when I was willing to be set free, God showed up BIG TIME in my behalf and walked me to freedom!

Prayer for the Day

Thank you, Father God, for caring about all the little details of our lives. Thank you that YOU ARE OUR SELF-CONTROL when we give You the reins of our lives. Amen!

The Game of Discipline

I appeal to you therefore, brethren, by the mercies of God, to present your bodies as a living sacrifice, holy and acceptable unto God, which is your spiritual worship."
Romans 12:1 (RSV)

Most of us can probably quote that scripture without any problem, but as we commit our lives to Christ and give Him the right to change us from the inside out, it is totally necessary to depend upon the discipline of the Holy Spirit.

Within a few months after I quit smoking, I had gained so much weight that I weighed the same as I did the day our second daughter was born - while I was still pregnant! Boy! Was I disgusted with myself! One morning during my prayer time, I was pouring my heart out to God. I sensed Him saying to me, "Who lives inside you?" "You do," was my answer. "What does that make you?"

I got up from my chair and walked to the mirror. Standing in front of it, I said, "Jesus Christ lives inside me. That makes me beautiful because He is beautiful!"

The Lord and I began to learn to eat properly. Praying about everything I put in my mouth became a way of life for me. I would open the refrigerator and pray, "What shall I choose?" Long story short: by listening, being obedient and retraining my appetite, I lost 55 pounds in one year. Of course, it wasn't just eating properly but also exercising along the way.

Self-control comes with much practice, patience, and discipline. Take one day at a time, listen carefully to the voice of the Holy Spirit within you, and be willing to re-train yourself in whatever area you may need extra strength.

Prayer for the Day

Thank you, Father, You never ask us to do anything You won't help us accomplish! Amen!

Guard My Mouth

"Set a guard over my mouth, O Lord, keep watch over the door of my lips!"
Psalm 141:3 (RSV)

Oh, my as we consider self-control, the mouth has to be a great part of our discipline. Our pastor, Peter Lord, told us one time, "It's my mouth that causes me the most trouble - what goes into it and what comes out of it." Of course, we all laughed, but there's much truth to that statement. Laughter often softens pain.

My problem in eating properly was learning what to put into my mouth. I prayed daily and at every meal preparation. The Lord told me to eat a grapefruit before every meal in 1970 - before the world was doing a "grapefruit diet." Living in Florida, I never had to buy any! Friends would drop them by my house by the sack full without my telling anyone what I was doing. I ate one half before each meal without any sugar, of course.

I also had to eat three times a day, which was real discipline for me because I had been a breakfast skipper and a major snacker with cokes all day. I lost my appetite for cokes - maybe because of the grapefruit - and began to drink large amounts of water of all things!

Step by step He led me as I listened for instruction. What went into my mouth changed drastically and so did my health! You see, I wasn't on a diet; I was being trained in a new way of living. PTL!

Prayer for the Day

Thank you, Father, You care about every detail of our lives - even what we put into our bodies. Amen!

Broken City

"A man without self-control is like a city broken into and left without walls."
Proverbs 25:28 (RSV)

As we read yesterday in Ps. 141:3, we saw God wants us to guard our lips. In training me to eat properly, the Lord taught me a powerful lesson. I discovered as I reached for snacks, many times it was to satisfy a frustration in my life - anger, fear, weariness, etc. I began to realize I was using food to quench a hunger in my spirit.

Growing up in East Tennessee, we were taught to clean our plates and never leave anything behind. I'm certain some of that came from our parents and grandparents surviving the Depression years. However, any time I was upset, someone would offer me something to eat to settle me. We do that with babies, you know, as we give them a bottle just to satisfy them even when they may not be hungry.

Because of my personality, I needed great oral satisfaction - grab a bite, drink a coke, chew gum, etc. During my "training camp" year in learning to eat properly, I began to grasp in frustration I needed to turn to the Lord.

"Hey, Father, I'm so angry! Help my anger. Heal my hurt." or "Lord, please allow me peace in the midst of this aggravation." You get the picture, I'm sure.

As I turned to constant communication with God, my insatiable desire for food satisfaction changed to a fresh knowledge of WHO HE IS IN ME!

The process has continued through the years as many challenges have come my way, but He has never disappointed me!

Prayer for the Day

Thank you, Father, for walking at my right hand, leading me toward freedom in every area of my life. I want to be a strong city, fortified with Your life in me! Amen!

Touch of the Master's Hand

*"And he touched my mouth, and said:
'Behold, this has touched your lips;
your guilt is taken away, and your sin forgiven.'"*
Isaiah 6:7 (RSV)

When Isaiah saw the Lord, his life was changed forever as was each of ours. I'm certain as he walked the streets where he was called, he too had opportunity to feel guilty, but look at the power the hot coal gave his mouth. He prophesied the coming of Messiah!

When I make wrong choices in my eating or speaking, I think of this verse. The hot coal of the Lord God Almighty has changed my mouth - giving me the power to resist temptation, forgiving me of all my guilt and shame, and granting me the freedom to practice what He has shown me to do.

One day I had a big argument with a bag of jelly beans, which was one of my favorite indulgences. Anyway, the bag was on the kitchen counter and beckoned me to eat. At first I said, "No, I don't want to eat you," because I knew I couldn't eat just a couple, but I'd go for the whole bag. Inside I knew I had lied because I *really did want to eat them.*

So, I changed my words, "Okay. I do want to eat you, but I'm only going to eat five of you. You do not rule my life! In the Name of the Lord Jesus Christ, I have power to withstand any and all temptation." So, I ate a few and walked away, which was a major milestone in my conquering my mouth and the cravings in my life. Over and over I've remembered that moment and have argued with other temptations in the same manner, taking control of my life as well as my mouth. The Name of Jesus Christ is a powerful weapon against which no foe can stand.

Prayer for the Day

Father, thank you when we're honest with You, Your power is limitless in our lives. Amen!

Guard Your Throat

*"When you sit down to eat with a ruler,
observe carefully what is before you;
and put a knife to your throat if you
are a man given to appetite."*
Proverbs 23:1-2 (RSV)

Through the years I read the book of Proverbs through each month (There are 31 chapters, so it's a perfect devotional). Well, during the years of training my appetite, this particular scripture had great impact on my choices in foods.

When we are eating out or with friends or family, often people want you to eat items that may not be particularly healthy for your body. This verse of scripture comes to my mind over and over. My body reacts to certain food items which cause me health issues, so I've learned to decline rather than pay the price of a headache or unusual swelling. Sometimes this has been difficult for others to accept. However, one must set boundaries when he knows what is good for him.

I've learned to say, "Thank you very much, but could I have more of 'this dish' instead." That way no one is offended and explanations are unnecessary. I also ask myself, even though I may want to eat something, if I'm willing to pay with the results. That often helps me decide to practice self-control because I use to get caught in the trap of thinking, "just this once," but there are usually consequences.

Prayer for the Day

Thank you, Father, Your Spirit is stronger than any temptation that comes my way, whether it is food or any other craving that is unhealthy for me. Fill me afresh today so that I may make God choices along the way. Amen!

Bridle the Tongue

"If any one thinks he is religious, and does not bridle his tongue but deceives his heart, this man's religion is vain."
James 1:26 (RSV)

James left us such incredible insight to following hard after God in our daily lives, and with this one statement, his writing has certainly challenged my self-control. Just when I think I may have something "all together" a situation occurs causing me to open my big mouth with a sharp answer or a word out of season.

As I commented earlier, our pastor in Florida said, "My mouth is my biggest problem - what goes into it and what comes out of it." Both are extremely challenging, but for me the taming of the tongue has been quite the journey.

Certainly we don't want to come across as "know it all's." However, with my thirty some years of teaching school, my authoritative voice often comes across to people as though I'm chief in charge. The Lord is working on me to soften my quick answers, to change the tone in which I speak and to think before I open my mouth. Needless to say, this is an on-going process as I learn to trust the Holy Spirit daily to fill me, to rekindle my life, and to draw me unto the likeness of Jesus Christ.

Prayer for the Day

Father, thank you for teaching me not to be so quick to judge others! Help me to take control of my tongue in the power of the Holy Spirit within me to gain self-control over my mouth! Amen!

Small Member

"If we put bits into the mouths of horses that they may obey us, we guide their whole bodies. . . So the tongue is a little member and boasts of great things. How great a forest is set ablaze by a small fire!"
James 3:3 & 5 (RSV)

Well, now, self-control becomes an extremely important fruit when we consider we must be the master of our tongue if our mouth goes in the right direction. So many times words have flown out of my mouth that I couldn't believe! The old saying, "Sticks and stones may break my bones, but words can never hurt me" just isn't the truth. We have all been wounded by words spoken in anger or given for purposes other than goodness.

When I was filled with the Holy Spirit in 1970 sitting at our dining room table, the very first sign I received was that I no longer needed those foul four-letter words that had been a part of my daily vocabulary. Suddenly, they left me. If found myself saying "Glory!" or "Hallelujah!" or "Praise the Lord!" instead of using foul language. It was such a freedom that I knew God had touched me and was in the process of making me whole from the inside out.

That was a miraculous deliverance. I wish I could say the control of that little part of my body was an easy thing in other areas, but I've had to practice, apologize, restate things, go back to ask forgiveness, and repent to the Lord God for words spoken unjustly. He's still working on me forty years later to let my words be few and tender to those around me.

Prayer for the Day

Lord Jesus, thank you for Your example of controlling Your words in the earth. Thank you that You brought many people to Yourself with Your gentleness, grace, and speaking the truth in love. Please help me to be a carrier of peace upon my tongue. Amen!

Life

Death and life are in the power of the tongue, and those who love it will eat its fruits."
Proverbs 18:21 (RSV)

Wow! LIFE is in the power of the tongue! What a privilege for us as believers to have at our lip-tips. The verse preceding this says *"From the fruit of his mouth a man is satisfied; he is satisfied by the yield of his lips." (Prov. 18:22)* So if I have the power to control my lips through the fruit of self-control and the power of the Holy Spirit, then I have the strength to practice what Proverbs is teaching.

When Johnny had open-heart surgery in 1995, we were told his chances of living were slim because of where the blockage was in his heart. However, we sang songs, confessed scripture, settled peaceful life decisions, and believed God for LIFE to surround Johnny with the goodness of God at his side. Now here we are over 14 years later and we're still declaring LIFE!

Has every day been filled with what we would call "perfect health" in the natural? No, not really. However, LIFE giving power from on high has been available to Johnny as well as to me throughout the journey. LIFE is a way to travel safely through whatever journey comes our way. Nothing can stop the resurrected power of Jesus Christ in our lives if we choose to speak life for ourselves along the way.

Then no matter what the outcome, we continue on with LIFE at every turn in our journey. GOD IS THE LIFE GIVER! Speaking HIS WORDS gives us LIFE!

Prayer for the Day

Thank you, Father, for giving us the freedom to choose LIFE and LIFE MORE ABUNDANTLY! Amen!

Speak Life

> *"And to this people you shall say: 'Thus says the Lord: Behold, I set before you the way of life and the way of death.'"*
> **Jeremiah 21:8 (RSV)**

When we consider our choices for each day to choose the great life in God or the way of the world, we are reminded that God Himself told us to choose life. He was telling the people to leave the city because God had set His face against the city where they were. Now, what we have to realize is that God knew the GOOD PLANS for the lives of the people so He knew where they needed to be.

When we choose to follow the LIFE of God, He will direct our paths. He has plans for good and not evil all the days of our lives *(Jeremiah. 29:11)*. In order to choose the God way of life, we must learn to bridle our tongues in speaking good things over our lives and the lives of our children as well as their children. God will fill our mouths with good speech as we choose to walk in His way, declaring His works, and expecting His blessing because we follow after Him.

Determine in your heart to speak positively and watch God carry goodness everywhere you go.

Prayer for the Day

Thank you, Father, for giving us the privilege of choosing the good life, walking in Your light, and trusting in Your way. Forgive me where I have doubted. I choose to speak faith words today! Amen!

Gracious Speech

*Let your speech always be gracious, seasoned
with salt, so that you may know
how you ought to answer every one."*
Colossians 4:6 (RSV)

How many times have I opened my mouth and let the words fly out before I thought through what should be said? Especially in anger, it is easy to say things we wish we could take back, but once they're out of the mouth, they are gone if the hearer was there. Self-control teaches us to allow the Holy Spirit to heal us before we lash out at others with whatever goes through the brain first. We've all known many people who just say whatever is on their minds - not always a healthy thing to do to others.

To allow my speech to be gracious and seasoned with salt (life-giving power), I must step back and wait for the right moment to present itself and the right words to fill my mouth for a response. Quite often, no response is needed. That's the most difficult for me because I always want to use words. Through the years, I have learned to wait upon the Lord to answer back or even give unwanted advice to others. Not that I always respond in the right way, but I am practicing because even though I was always told "Sticks and stones may break my bones, but words can never hurt me," I know words do hurt! If I wait on the Lord and on His power to work through me, hopefully my words can be healing, calming, life-giving, and full of love.

Prayer for the Day

Thank you, Lord, for making us instruments of Your peace. Where there is hatred, let us sow love. Just like St. Francis, please allow us the privilege of being gracious to others at all times. Amen!

Public Self-Control

*". . . let us consider how to stir up one
another to love and good works . . ."*
Hebrews 10:24 (RSV)

Yesterday I had a marvelous opportunity to practice self-control in a bookstore. Another lady and I walked up to the register at the same time - she was just a step or two behind me. There were a couple of people ahead of us, so we waited. I sensed she was extremely anxious for some reason, so when my turn came, I asked her if she'd like to go first. She was amazed!

Then as she took care of her purchase, she shared, "My son just called me to say he wanted to spend time with me before I leave tomorrow for one month. I told him I would hurry, so thank you so very much for being so patient."

In appropriating the self-control of the Holy Spirit and considering others more important than myself at that moment, I was able to bless another believer who was trusting God for precious time with her son. God knows the needs of those around us if we're sensitive to His voice. After all, we have time. God is not in a hurry when it comes to treating others with kindness, patience, small gifts, and love.

As I went on my way, three other opportunities came to me in other places. In hearing and obeying, the Lord blessed several through me during their harried day. We are peace to the world around us!

Prayer for the Day

Thank you, Father, for granting me the self-control not to be consumed with my own needs that I miss the needs in others. Help me encourage others in love! Amen!

Practicing the Walk

Little children, let us not love in word or speech but in deed and in truth."

I John 3:18 (RSV)

As we wrap up our look at the fruit of the Spirit, I thought the testimony from one of our readers is a perfect example of love, joy, peace, patience, kindness, goodness, faithfulness, gentleness and self-control.

A living testimony from today's world:

"Your devotional reminded me of what happened to me a few days ago. I had driven to Hendersonville to meet my sister and pick up my nieces to bring them here for camp. We were eating lunch at a Cracker Barrel, and I kept being drawn to an elderly man sitting alone at a table across the aisle. I began to feel compassion toward him, and sensed I needed to go speak to him. The usual thoughts ran through my mind - Will he think I'm nuts? What will my family think when I go talk to a complete stranger? The urgency I felt grew stronger, so ignoring my negative thoughts, I acted in obedience and went over to speak to the man. The Lord brought to my remembrance that this man reminded me of a dear friend's father who had been special in my life, so that gave me some opening comments. As our conversation progressed, he told me he was there alone because his wife was beginning chemo treatments for cancer that very day. She had been very healthy and the diagnosis came as a complete shock to them. I asked him for her

name, and told him I would pray for her. I was able to speak words of encouragement to this man, and I could see he was deeply moved. I was flooded with a sense that Jesus wanted to show love and compassion to this man, and I was so humbled and thankful to be used by Him. A little later, the Lord gave me an opportunity to help a lady in the restroom with her elderly mother-in-law, and it was pure joy to me."

Thus we walk.

Prayer for the Day

Thank you, Lord God, as we walk upon the earth, we can pour out our lives with Your Spirit in us to show the goodness of the Lord God in the land of the living. Amen!

Closing Thoughts from the Author

The Abundant Life

In 1970 Rev. Peter Lord taught our mid-week outreach study called "Savior 70" at Park Avenue Baptist Church in Titusville, Florida. In May of that year the Holy Spirit had filled my life, healed my body from migraine headaches, and set my life on a path of love, joy, peace, patience, kindness, faithfulness, gentleness, and self-control. The changes have taken place progressively through the years, and according to Philippians 1:6 the Lord will continue to work in my life until I meet Him in the air – whenever that might come. In one of the devotionals, I shared how God had used the infilling of the Holy Spirit to teach me about patience with my children. Now I'd like to share the steps that brought me to this life of abundant living each day.

1. In 1958 I prayed to receive Jesus Christ as my Savior in Jonesborough United Methodist Church at a revival led by Rev. Russell. At that moment love flooded my life so that God drew me into the study of His Word and a hunger to know Him more.

SIMPLE PRAYER: *Lord God, I have sinned against you. Forgive me of any wrong in my life to cleanse me and make me whole. I accept Jesus Christ as my Savior and Lord by receiving Him into my heart to live with me forever. Amen!*

Truly, salvation is that simple. John 3:16 promises us God gave His only Son so that we might know Him, love Him, and be changed by Him. Powerful truth of His great love for each of us!

2. In 1968 John Russell and I became man and wife in Honolulu, Hawaii. Our first major decision was we would always have prayer before every meal and never forget to thank God Almighty for the blessing of bringing our lives together. Secondly, we decided to never eat in front of a television, but to sit at our table to use the time to share life together with one another and later our family. We continue to base our lives on that decision in 2009. The peace of God and the focus on Who is at our table has kept us thinking about our Father each day.

3. In 1970 I was introduced to the living Holy Spirit. Even though I had declared, "I believe in the Father, Son and the Holy Spirit," I did not understand the work of the Holy Spirit upon the face of the earth. When the understanding of the gift of the Holy Spirit to every believer became truth to me, I knew Jesus had come not only to give me resurrection life in the sweet by-and-by, but He had also made a way for me to have the Holy Spirit alive in me so that I could

live victoriously in the nasty now-and-now. This powerful truth has never failed me, so I want to share those steps with you in scripture with the hope that you as well will experience the fullest, greatest, most peaceful life each day.

a. Natural Person (One who has not received Christ): I Corinthians 2:14 – *But the natural, nonspiritual man does not accept or welcome or admit into his heart the gifts and teachings and revelations of the Spirit of God, for they are folly (meaningless nonsense) to him; and he is incapable of knowing them [of progressively recognizing, understanding, and becoming better acquainted with them] because they are spiritually discerned and estimated and appreciated.* (AMP)

b. Spiritual Person (One who is directed and empowered by the Holy Spirit): I Corinthians 2:15-16 – *But the spiritual man tries all things [he examines, investigates, inquires into, questions, and discerns all things], yet is himself to be put on trial and judged by no one [he can read the meaning of everything, but no one can properly discern or appraise or get an insight into him].* [16]*For who has known or understood the mind (the counsels and purposes) of the Lord so as to guide and instruct Him and give Him knowledge? But we have the mind of Christ (the Messiah) and do hold the thoughts (feelings and purposes) of His heart.* (AMP)

    c. John 10:10 – *The thief comes only in order to steal and kill and destroy. I came that they may have and enjoy life, and have it in abundance (to the full, till it overflows). (AMP)*

    d. John 15:5 – *I am the Vine; you are the branches. Whoever lives in Me and I in him bears much (abundant) fruit. However, apart from Me [cut off from vital union with Me] you can do nothing. (AMP)*

    e. Galatians 5:22-23 – *But the fruit of the [Holy] Spirit [the work which His presence within accomplishes] is love, joy (gladness), peace, patience (an even temper, forbearance), kindness, goodness (benevolence), faithfulness, [23]Gentleness (meekness, humility), self-control (self-restraint, continence). Against such things there is no law [that can bring a charge].* (AMP)

    f. Acts 1:8 – *But you shall receive power (ability, efficiency, and might) when the Holy Spirit has come upon you, and you shall be My witnesses in Jerusalem and all Judea and Samaria and to the ends (the very bounds) of the earth.* (AMP)

One becomes a Christian through the ministry of the Holy Spirit according to John 3:1-8. From the moment we receive Christ as our Savior, believers are indwelt by the Holy Spirit at all times (John 1:12; Colossians 2:9-10; John 14:16-17). However, though believers are indwelt by the Holy Spirit, not all know how to appropriate His power in their daily lives. That's where I was in 1970. Even though He lived in me, I didn't know how to dwell in, rely on, and trust in Him.

The Holy Spirit is the source of an overflowing life according to John 7:37-39. He came to glorify Christ in John 16:1-15 to help make us true disciples of Jesus. Christ commanded us in Acts 1:1-9 to be filled with the Holy Spirit so that we can be witnesses for Him on the face of the earth. Since that was His last command, it must be fairly significant!

Anyone can appropriate the filling of the Holy Spirit anywhere any time when 1) he/she sincerely desires to be directed and empowered by the Holy Spirit (Matthew 5:6; John 7:37-39). 2) One confesses his/her sins and by faith thanks God that He has forgiven all – past, present, and future (Colossians 2:13-15; I John 1; 2:1-3; Hebrews 10:1-17). 3) One presents every area of his/her life to God (Romans 12:1-2). 4) By faith he/she claims the fullness of the Holy Spirit according to Ephesians 5:18 and I John 5:14-15.

Once I was convinced the Word of the Lord was clear about the gift of the Holy Spirit, the next step was easy for me. It became a matter of a faith prayer to declare I believed it because God had promised it so I sat down at my dining room table one afternoon after I'd put my two little girls down for their afternoon nap.

1. I made a list of all the sins in my life I could do nothing about – bitterness toward my past, unforgiveness toward members of my family, doubts in God, hurts I'd never put to rest,

my own insecurity, my hatred for some folks who had wronged me, and my own sins of commission as well as omission. Then I asked God to forgive me of all the things on that list. I knew I couldn't do anything about them. I tore the list into pieces and cannot even remember all that was on it. As I ripped it to shreds, I knew God was cleansing my life.

2. The lady who shared these truths with me had said, "God cannot fill a dirty vessel, but He'll never leave a clean vessel empty." I believed her!

3. I prayed a prayer to be filled with the Holy Spirit:

Father, I cannot do anything about all these things. I need you to cleanse me of all my sins. Come into my life, clean my heart and soul, and fill me with Your blessed Holy Spirit! You told me it was a free gift. I accept the Holy Spirit totally into my life. Thank you for filling my life and making me whole right now. Amen!

Well, believe it or not, there were no fireworks. Time didn't stop. Lights came on in me that I didn't know were possible. Suddenly I was filled with this great peace that passed anything I'd ever experienced before. Sitting at that table my life was totally transformed! The four-letter words that had been a part of my everyday vocabulary dropped away to be replaced by "Glory to God!" "Praise the Lord!" or "Hallelujah!" The joy in my home was everywhere I turned – in my singing to my girls, in my cooking, in my cleaning, in my life with my wonderful husband, in every aspect of life. Studying the Word of God became such a joy as the words on the pages came to life in me. After all, the Holy Spirit is the Teacher inside us and He opened a whole new world of freedom for me and my family!

In that course of "Savior 70" I took, Peter Lord taught us his <u>959 Plan</u>, which is a plan designed to study the Word of God each day and pray the Word of God for nine minutes and fifty-nine seconds each day. He taught us to read the scripture, write down our thoughts God was giving us individually for the day before beginning our prayer time. In prayer, he taught us to 1) give thanks, 2) give praise, 3) make our requests for others known to God, 4) intercede for our nation and world, and 5) make our own petitions for ourselves. Through the years my discovery has been that as I pray for others, my needs are fully met. We wrote our thoughts on scripture and then we wrote our prayers, keeping track of prayers answered by our Father. God is good! That list of answers grew and grew, but the most important part was that my life was changed. God's Word was truly a light unto my path and His presence within me was my power source for each day.

Life has never been the same. Walking with Father, Son and Holy Spirit has been an adventure over the past decades. My love for them has grown as the truth of their power, love, authority, and fulfillment has come alive in me. There is no other way to live! Come join the ride and enjoy every day of your own personal lives filled with His goodness and lost in His love!

Dava Lee Russell, an ordained minister and founder of DLR Ministries, has lived the principles throughout the pages of this book for over forty years. As both a public school educator and bible teacher she has empowered students and adults to achieve their personal dreams and ambitions. In addition to foreign mission work and publications, she facilitates regional bible studies and retreats, sharing the realities of growing into the nature of Christ through her own personal journey as a believer. The life lessons she has captured are evidence of the power to live in the abundant Christian life.

Publications by Author

<u>A Family's Heritage</u>, Stories From Main Street Jonesborough (1996)

Study Guides	**CD Teaching Sets Available**
The Tabernacle	*Preparation of the Bride*
Preparation of the Bride	*Follow Hard After God*
Follow Hard After God	*Living the Spirit-Filled Life*
Living the Spirit-Filled Life	*Living in Kingdom Power*
Living in Kingdom Power	*Freedom!*
Freedom!	*The Way of the Eagle*
The Way of the Eagle	*The Battle Is the Lord's*
The Battle Is the Lord's	*Intimacy with the Father*
Intimacy with the Father	*Walking in Victory Every Day*
Walking in Victory Every Day	*Philippians*
Philippians	*Standing Strong in the Battle*
How the Bible Came to Be	
Dwelling Safely in Troubled Times	

Materials may be obtained from
<u>www.davaleerussellministries.org</u> or writing:
    Dava Lee Russell Ministries
    P. O. Box 231
    Jonesborough, TN 37659-0231
For more copies of <u>Fruitful Living</u>, contact <u>www.authorhouse.com</u>